NGOs:

Formation & Resource Mobilization

NGOs:

Formation & Resource Mobilization

Puran Chandra

AKANSHA PUBLISHING HOUSE
NEW DELHI - 110 002 (INDIA)

AKANSHA PUBLISHING HOUSE
4649/21-B, Ansari Road
Daryaganj, New Delhi - 110 002
Phones: 23263193, 9811582579
E-mail: ektabooks@yahoo.com

NGOs: Formation & Resource Mobilization

First Published, 2007

ISBN 978-81-8370-105-1

PRINTED IN INDIA

Published by M.P. Misra for Akansha Publishing House, New Delhi - 110 002 and Printed at Capital Offset Press, Delhi

Contents

Preface

As of now, NGOs have become major players in the field of international development. Since the mid-1970s, the NGO sector in both developed and developing countries has experienced exponential growth. In 1992 international NGOs channeled over $7.6 billion of aid to developing countries. It is now estimated that over 15 percent of total overseas development aid is channeled through NGOs. While statistics about global numbers of NGOs are incomplete, it is currently estimated that there is somewhere between 6,000 and 30,000 national NGOs in developing countries. CBOs (i.e. community-based organisations) across the developing world number in the hundreds of thousands.

NGOs are defined (in technical terms) by the World Bank as "private organizations that pursue activities to relieve suffering, promote the interests of the poor, protect the environment, provide basic social services, or undertake community development" (Operational Directive 14.70). In more wider context, the term NGO can be applied to any non-profit organization which is independent from government. NGOs arc typically value-based organizations which depend, in whole or in part, on charitable donations and voluntary service. As such also known as voluntary organisations. Although the NGO sector has become increasingly professionalized over the last two decades, principles of altruism and voluntarism remain key defining characteristics.

The NGO is a nebulous term and is very broad and encompasses many different types of organizations within its fold. In the field of development, NGOs range from large, Northern-based charities such as CARE, Oxfam and World Vision to community-based self-help groups in the South. They also include research institutes, churches, professional associations and lobby groups. The World Bank tends to interact with two main categories of NGOs: i) *operational* NGOs — whose primary purpose is the design and implementation of development-related projects, and; ii) *advocacy* NGOs — whose primary purpose is to defend or promote a specific cause and who seek to influence the policies and practices of the Bank. It should be noted, however, that these two categories are not mutually exclusive. A growing number of NGOs engage in both operational and advocacy activities, and some advocacy groups, while not directly involved in designing and implementing projects, focus on specific project-related topics.

As per the World Bank classification operational NGOs are grouped as: (a) *community-based* organizations (CBOs) - which serve a specific population in a narrow geographic area; (b) *national* organizations - which operate in individual developing countries, and; (c) *international* organizations - which are typically headquartered in developed countries and carry out operations in more than one developing country. Throughout the 1970s and 1980s, most examples of World Bank-NGO collaboration involved international NGOs. In recent years, however, this trend has been reversed. Among projects involving NGO collaboration recorded in FY94, 40% involved CBOs, 70% involved national organizations and 10% involved international organizations.

It is remarkable to note that are distinct in nature and

purpose from other NGOs. While national and international organizations are "intermediary" NGOs which are formed to serve others; CBOs are normally "membership" organizations made up of a group of individuals who have joined together to further their own interests (e.g.: women's groups, credit circles, youth clubs, cooperatives and farmer associations). In the context of Bank-financed activities, national or international NGOs are normally contracted to deliver services, design projects or conduct research. CBOs are more likely to be the recipients of project goods and services. In projects which promote participatory development, grassroots organizations play the key function of providing an institutional framework for beneficiary participation. Many national and international NGOs work in partnership with CBOs - either channeling development resources to them or providing them with services or technical assistance. Such NGOs can play a particularly important role as "intermediaries" between CBOs and institutions such as the World Bank or any government at national level.

Remarkably, 'Individual operational NGOs' vary enormously according to their purpose, philosophy, sectoral expertise and scope of activities. NGOs have been classified according to whether they are more relief or development-oriented; whether they are religious or secular; whether they stress service delivery or participation and whether they are more public or private-oriented.

Since the nature and quality of individual NGOs varies greatly, it is extremely difficult to make generalizations about the sector as a whole. In spite of this diversity, some specific strengths generally associated with the NGO sector include the following:

- strong grassroots links;

- field-based development expertise;
- the ability to innovate and adapt;
- process-oriented approach to development;
- participatory methodologies and tools;
- long-term commitment and emphasis on sustainability;
- cost-effectiveness.

On the other hand, the most commonly identified weaknesses of the sector include: limited financial and management expertise; limited institutional capacity; low levels of self-sustainability; isolation/lack of inter-organizational communication and/or coordination; small scale interventions; lack of understanding of the broader social or economic context.

NGOs rely on funding from individual donors, foundations, corporations and governments. Critics charge that funding sources can seriously affect NGO policy, making these organizations potentially the creatures of special interests. Such charges challenge NGO legitimacy especially when funds come from "outside" — including rich foreign governments, corporations or foundations.

Keeping in view the importance of NGOs as partners/ participants in delivering various developmental/relief services to the needy all over the world, it is important to gather basic information regarding NGO formation and resource mobilization, in particular reference to our country—India. Though instances have been taken from other countries too.

This book consists of the following topics, namely—NGOs: An Overview; NGO Formation: Procedure & Practices; Fund-raising in Developing Countries: Basic

Guidelines; NGOs and Conflict Resolution; NGOs and Financing Dilemma; NGO Perspectives on the Global Fund: A Report; NGO Participation in National AIDS Control Program: Basic Guidelines; and Starting Nonprofit Organization in US and Relevant Issues etc.

The text of major rules and regulations to be followed is reproduced for ready reference. An exhaustive bibliography and list of acronyms and glossary are added features of the book.

Admittedly, work(s) of this nature can be presented in proper sequence, obtaining help and guidance from expert lines. As such, entire credit for this ought go to original contributors, on whose research findings this book substantially based. The help, assistance and guidance received from various corners is duly acknowledged. Finally, are owe a deep sense of gratitude to Mr. M.P. Misra for bringing out this volume.

—Editor

Acronyms

AIMS	Assessing the Impact of Microenterprise Services
CBO	Community Based Organisation
CDIE	Centre for Development Information and Evaluation
CEM	Centro de Estudias de la Mujer (Centre for Women's Studies)
CHW	Community Health Worker
CIDA	Canadian International Development Agency
CIDE	Centro de Investigacion y Desarrollo de la Educacion (Centre for Education Research and Development)
CONGAD	Conseil des ONG d'appui au développement
DAC	Development Assistance Committee
DAI	Development Alternatives Incorporated
DANIDA	Danish International Development Agency
DCA	DanChurchAid
DFID	Department for International Development
DIS	Diakonhjemmets Internasjonale Senter
EC	European Commission
EU	European Union
FVS	Finnish Volunteer Service

GAO	General Audit Office
GOM	Gemeenschappelijk Overleg Medefinanciering
GRET	Groupe de recherche et d'échanges technologiques
HPD	Health and Population Division
IDS	Institute of Development Studies
IEC	Information, Education and Communication
IEP	Instituto de Ecologia Politica (Institute for Political Ecology)
INDAP	Instituto para el Desarrollo Agropecuario (Agricultural Development Institute)
KEPA	The Service Centre for Development Cooperation (Finland)
K-REP	Kenya Rural Enterprise Programme
MBP	Microenterprise Best Practice
MIP	Microenterprise Innovation Project
NCA	Norwegian Church Aid
NGO	Non-Governmental Organisation
NORAD	Norwegian Agency for Development Cooperation
ODA	Overseas Development Administration
ODI	Overseas Development Institute
OECD	Organisation for Economic Cooperation and Development
OPVC	Office of Private Voluntary Cooperation
ORT	Oral Rehydration Therapy
PME	Project appraisal, Monitoring and Evaluation
PVO	Private Voluntary Organisation

REMAPP	NGO Group on Research and Evaluation (UK)
SEEP	Small Enterprise Educational and Promotional Network
Sida	Swedish International Development Authority
SIDA	Swedish International Development Cooperation Agency
SODECAM	Sociedad para el Desarrollo del Campesino Mapuche (Society for the Development of the Mapuche Peasant)
TOR	Terms of Reference
UK	United Kingdom
UK/I	United Kingdom and Ireland
US	United States
USAID	United States Agency for International Development

1

NGOs: An Overview

NGO, i.e. non-governmental organization is widely popular term these days known and understood as such all over the world barring all barriers — linguistic, racial, national, regional or whatever may be, which have proved instrumental in various developmental and emergency activities.

The term non-governmental organization (NGO) is used in a variety of ways all over the world and, depending on the context in which it is used, can refer to many different types of organizations. In its broadest sense, a non-governmental organization is one that is not directly part of the structure of government. Anheier places the number of internationally operating NGOs at 40,000 (Anheier et al, "Global Civil Society 2001", 2001). National numbers are even higher: The United States has an estimated 2 million NGOs, most of them formed in the past 30 years. Russia has 4,000 NGOs. India is estimated to have between 1 and 2 million or more NGOs.

International Red Cross and Red Crescent Movement is the world's largest group of humanitarian NGOs. Though voluntary associations of citizens have existed throughout history, NGOs along the lines seen today, especially on the international level, have developed in the past two centuries.

One of the first such organizations, the International Committee of the Red Cross, was founded in 1863.

Remarkably, the term non-governmental organization (NGO) was not in general currency before the UN was formed. When 132 international NGOs decided to co-operate with each other in 1910, they did so under the label, the 'Union of International Associations'. The League of Nations officially referred to its "liaison with private organizations", while many of these bodies at that time called themselves international institutes, international unions or simply international organizations. The first draft of the UN Charter did not make any mention of maintaining co-operation with private bodies. A variety of groups, mainly but not solely from the USA, lobbied to rectify this at the San Francisco conference, which established the UN in 1945. Not only did they succeed in introducing a provision for strengthening and formalizing the relations with private organizations previously maintained by the League, they also greatly enhanced the UN's role in economic and social issues and upgraded the status of the Economic and Social Council (ECOSOC) to a "principal organ" of the UN. To clarify matters, new terminology was introduced to cover ECOSOC's relationship with two types of international organizations. Under Article 70, "specialized agencies, established by intergovernmental agreement" could "participate without a vote in its deliberations", while under Article 71 "non-governmental organizations" could have "suitable arrangements for consultation". Thus, "specialized agencies" and "NGOs" became technical UN jargon. The term, NGO, passed into popular usage, particularly from the early 1970s onwards.

Globalization during the last decade of 20th century with increasing intensity during dawn of the 21st century gave rise to the importance of NGOs. Many problems could not be solved within a nation. International treaties and international organizations such as the World Trade Organization were perceived as being too centred on the interests of capitalist enterprises. In an attempt to counterbalance this trend, NGOs have developed to emphasize humanitarian issues, developmental aid and sustainable development. A prominent example of this is the World Social Forum which is a rival convention to the World Economic Forum held annually in January in Davos, Switzerland. The fifth World Social Forum in Porto Alegre, Brazil, in January 2005 was attended by representatives from more than 1,000 NGOs.

In fact, so far there is no generally accepted definition of an NGO and the term carries different connotations in different context. Nevertheless, there are some fundamental features. Clearly an NGO must be independent from the direct control of any government. In addition, there are three other generally accepted characteristics that exclude particular types of bodies from consideration. An NGO will not be constituted as a political party; it will be non-profit-making and it will be not be a criminal group, in particular it will be non-violent. These characteristics apply in general usage, because they match the conditions for recognition by the United Nations. The boundaries can sometimes be blurred: some NGOs may in practice be closely identified with a political party; many NGOs generate income from commercial activities, notably consultancy contracts or sales of publications; and a small number of NGOs may be associated with violent political protests. Nevertheless, an NGO is never constituted as a government bureaucracy, a party, a company, a criminal organization or a guerrilla group. Thus, for this article, an NGO is defined as an independent voluntary association of people acting together on a continuous basis, for some common purpose, other than achieving government office, making money or illegal activities.

Variously known as NGOs, Interest Groups, Pressure Groups, Lobbies and Private Voluntary Organizations etc. does NGO represent the same connotation.

In discussion of politics within countries, a distinction is often made between interest groups and pressure groups, but it is taken for granted that both types of private groups have an impact upon government policy-making. The term, interest group, is biased towards consideration of groups such as companies or trade unions. Use of the term is unsatisfactory, as it tends to imply that such groups are only concerned with economic policy, that they only act to safeguard their own economic position and that only groups with substantial economic resources can have an impact on politics. None of these propositions is valid. Major economic actors are also concerned with values beyond the accumulation of wealth. At the minimum, they also pursue security and status. At the maximum, they have a wider responsibility towards health and safety, social welfare and environmental values. The term, pressure group, invokes a wider range of groups. Its use is intended to cover those, such as environmentalists and human rights groups, who are pursuing goals that do not directly benefit themselves. It emphasizes the processes by which groups mobilize support to promote their political values. The contrast between interest groups and pressure groups can be used to suggest a contrast between objective goals and subjective goals and hence privilege the pursuit of economic returns over environmental values and other abstract values.

In America, a similar distinction is made, with stronger, but different, normative connotations. Mention of a lobby seems to imply the illegitimate use of wealth in a secretive manner, while private voluntary organizations or public interest groups convey a positive image. There is a logical problem with the distinction in that membership of a lobby is both private and voluntary. These terms are also unsatisfactory as the latter two suggest charitable activity and do not readily bring to mind campaigning groups nor those who are concerned with global issues, such as Greenpeace and Amnesty International. "Public interest" appears to cover the general good, in an objective manner, but it is an essentially-contested concept, both with respect to what is "the public" and with respect to identifying "the common interest". One person's view of the public interest may be seen by another person as the assertion of unacceptable values, ideological extremism or special pleading.

The distinction between interest groups and pressure groups or between lobbies and private voluntary organizations has no analytical value. All pressure groups or voluntary organizations have some interests to protect, even if it is only the maintenance of their reputation, increasing the number of active supporters and gaining sufficient income to communicate effectively. Altruistic charities use sophisticated public relations campaigns to raise funds and standard lobbying techniques when government taxation policy affects their income. Equally, all interest groups and lobbies are of political importance, precisely because their pressure influences social and political outcomes. They do not necessary operate in a secretive manner in the corridors of power and they do at times seek to mobilize public support. When they engage in political debate, company representatives often argue for general abstract values that go beyond their specific concrete interests. Companies can only challenge the public interest – or more precisely public opinion – at the risk of damaging their public reputation, their brand values and their income. Many companies more positively promote what is often seen as the public interest. They may donate profits to charitable activities, identify directly with environmental values to benefit from green consumerism or even reduce consumption of energy and raw materials to reduce costs. Trade unions usually go much further than companies in making explicit their endorsement of a wide range of political values. They also allocate money, personnel and other resources to campaigning, both independently and in coalition with other pressure groups.

Whatever one might think of these terms from the discourse on politics within countries, they are never used in global politics. Because diplomats like to claim that they are pursuing "the national interest" of a united society, they will not admit to relations with interest groups or pressure groups and they prefer the bland title, non-governmental organizations. The thinking behind the concept of a public interest group has been transferred to some people's attitudes to NGOs. There is a desire to limit access to the UN system to "proper" NGOs, but all this means is that groups supported by the person concerned should be included and other groups excluded. The other terms – interest group, pressure group, lobby and private voluntary organization – could *all* be applied legitimately to most NGOs. However, there is mutual connivance in most political processes at the global level to hide behind the uncontroversial catch-all term NGOs. The only significant exception, which is discussed below, is the tendency in global environmental politics to talk about "Major Groups". This sounds more positive, but it is still a vague term, devoid of any direct association with participation in policy-making.

In the logic of the language, there is no difference between a non-governmental organization and a private voluntary organization, but NGO still carries neutral connotations and applicability to a diverse range of political actors, whereas PVO suggests moral approval of a more limited range of groups. In practice, it is impossible to agree any general terms to distinguish praiseworthy from unacceptable groups, either in domestic politics or in global politics, because such a distinction is a subjective choice made on the basis of each observer's own value preferences.

In academic study of international relations, the term "transnational" was adopted to refer to any relationship across country boundaries, in which at least one of the actors was not a government. It was adopted in order to deny the assumption that international relations was the same as inter-state relations, or more precisely intergovernmental relations. It came into currency in the 1970s as a result of economic and environmental questions being recognized as a high priority for the global agenda. It is immediately apparent that the academic concept of a transnational actor is quite different from the political concept of an NGO. Firstly, it excludes all NGO activity that is confined to a single country. Secondly, it includes all the other non-governmental actors that have been defined as being outside the world of NGOs. It is commonplace to refer to transnational companies, transnational criminals, transnational guerrillas and transnational terrorists. In global politics, it is rare for any reference to be made to transnational NGOs, presumably because an NGO's involvement in global politics *ipso facto* makes it transnational.

Independence of NGOs

The most difficult question about the independence of

NGOs is whether they come under governmental influence. Individual governments do at times try to influence the NGO community in a particular field, by establishing NGOs that promote their policies. This has been recognized by quite common use of the acronym GONGO, to label a government-organized NGO. Also, in more authoritarian societies, NGOs may find it very difficult to act independently and they may not receive acknowledgment from other political actors even when they are acting independently. Beyond these unusual situations, there is a widespread prejudice that government funding leads to government control. In the field of human rights, it would damage an NGO for such a perception to arise, so Amnesty International has strict rules that it will not accept direct government funding for normal activities. On the other hand, development and humanitarian relief NGOs need substantial resources, to run their operational programs, so most of them readily accept official funds. While these NGOs would like the security of a guaranteed budget for their administrative overheads, governments generally only want to support field costs for projects.

Nominally NGOs may appear to be independent, when they design their own programs, but government influence can arise indirectly if the program is designed to make it more likely that government grants or contracts will be forthcoming. On the other hand, confident experienced NGOs can appeal for funding for new approaches and in so doing cause government officials to re-assess policy. The best example of this is the way in which NGOs, particularly the International Planned Parenthood Federation, dragged governments into adopting population programs. There is no obvious method to identify the direction of influence, without detailed knowledge of the relationship between an NGO and a government. Environmental NGOs may have either type of funding relationship. Conservation and research groups may happily obtain government funds to support their programs: some are innovative and some are not. Beyond these situations, radical campaigning groups may be unwilling and unable to attract government funds.

NGOs, Political Parties and Ethnic Minorities

It is remarkable that, while a political party is not regarded as an NGO and cannot gain recognition at the UN, a small number of transnational groupings of political parties do gain consultative status with ECOSOC. There are also several groups of parliamentarians with consultative status. No problems have arisen with either group, because they have carefully avoided trying to involve the UN in the "internal affairs of states". Human rights NGOs feel aggrieved that the same principle is applied to them, even though one of the purposes of ECOSOC is "promoting respect for, and observance of, human rights". In May 1968, ECOSOC Resolution 1296 (XLIV) specified that NGOs "should have a general international concern with this matter, not restricted to the interests of a particular group of persons, a single nationality or the situation in a single State". While this provision was dropped from the revised text in July 1996, it is still applied in practice. On this basis, the Indian government can block the World Sikh Organization from gaining UN recognition. Christian Solidarity International also lost its consultative status in October 1999 after it had allowed the guerrilla leader, John Garang, to speak on its behalf, at the Commission on Human Rights.

The recognition of minority rights is such a complex question that it is handled very differently in different countries. In both North and South America, the minority communities who are descendants of the inhabitants prior to the arrival of the great waves of European settlers are given the privileged title of "indigenous peoples". The term has also been adopted in Australia and New Zealand and a few other countries. On the other hand, governments in various ethnically diverse countries do not wish to accord any special recognition to minorities. The compromise is that the UN refers to indigenous people, as individuals who have rights, and not to indigenous peoples (note the plural). This avoids recognition of any collective identity or any claim to the right of self-determination. The restrictions deriving from Resolution 1296 mean the organizations with consultative status are mainly global or regional coalitions of ethnic minorities. However, special procedures have been adopted in both the Commission on Human Rights and the Commission on Sustainable Development to allow participation by a wider range of indigenous organizations. In addition, in July 2000, ECOSOC established a Permanent Forum on Indigenous Issues, consisting of sixteen independent experts, half of whom are nominated by indigenous organizations. Through a variety of complex issue linkages, these NGOs can be important in environmental politics, notably in the conservation of rainforests. While they are only present in the UN system under the auspices of the arrangements for NGOs, indigenous people are often keen to claim a unique status that is separate from and superior to the representatives of NGOs. As a result, their alliance with environmentalists does not always operate smoothly.

NGOs and their Relations with Business and Commerce

A few intergovernmental economic organizations do allow an individual company to have access under their provisions for NGOs, but this is only in cases where there are loose *ad hoc* procedures and there are no formal institutional arrangements. However, as with political parties, non-profit-making federations of companies, established for industry-wide collaboration and to act as lobbies, are widely accepted. From the earliest days of the UN, bodies such as the International Chamber of Commerce, the International Organization of Employers and similar organizations for particular economic sectors have been included among the NGOs. Until the 1990s, they were not of much significance in the UN itself, but they have always been important in the specialized agencies. The more technical the question under discussion, the more the policy-making process will draw on their expertise.

One of the outcomes of the 1992 Rio Earth Summit, the UN Conference on Environment and Development, was to draw companies into global environmental politics and hence more into the work of ECOSOC. Sectoral bodies are prominent when questions such as energy or transport are on the agenda. In addition, issue-oriented commercial grouping have been formed. The most prominent is the World Business Council for Sustainable Development, a successor to various lobbies that focused on the Earth Summit, to promote environmentally friendly business. The oil companies have sound environmental credentials in some forums, but not in others. The Oil Companies International Maritime Forum is making a useful contribution to the reduction of oil pollution at sea, but the Global Climate Coalition opposes reductions in oil consumption. OCIMF is registered as an NGO by the International Maritime Organization, and the GCC is admitted as an observer to the sessions of the Conference of the Parties to the Framework Convention on Climate Change.

At the World Economic Forum in Davos in January

1999, the UN Secretary-General, Kofi Annan, explicitly called upon companies to widen their social responsibilities by entering into a Global Compact with the UN. Companies that do so agree to endorse nine principles, covering promotion of a set of core values in the areas of human rights, labor standards and protection of the environment. Soon afterwards, global business organizations, several hundred companies and the International Confederation of Free Trade Unions responded positively, but only a handful of human rights, environment and development NGOs did so. There remains a deep suspicion among many such NGOs about the possibility of companies implementing commitments to social responsibility.

Despite the suspicion of business, some NGOs have chosen to engage directly in collaborative arrangements to formulate and monitor statements of business ethics. This has been done both on an industry-wide basis and with individual companies. For example, WWF took the lead in forming the Forest Stewardship Council in 1993 and the Marine Stewardship Council in 1996. Each Council works to promote sustainable practices, with participating companies gaining the benefit of having their products endorsed by the NGOs as being environmentally friendly. Similarly, various companies are having environmental and/or social audits undertaken on an annual basis, by independent assessors.

NGOs and the Political Use of Violence

There has been no compromise in any political system with the idea that the use of violence is not a normal part of the political process. In the UN, aggressive behavior by individuals is sufficient to raise the question of suspension of an NGO's consultative status. In the exceptional circumstances where group of guerrillas wish to claim their use of violence is acceptable as part of the struggle against an oppressive regime, the group does not call itself an NGO. Their supporters call them a national liberation movement, whereas their opponents call them terrorists. Sometimes these groups gain admittance to intergovernmental organizations, as if they were the governments of recognized states. At the UN, they have never been classified as NGOs, but a few have been given a different status, as observers at the General Assembly and at UN conferences. Within individual countries, there are rare examples of the use of violence as a deliberate tactic, by groups that would normally be referred to as NGOs. A clear example is the Animal Liberation Front in the United Kingdom. They are simply regarded as criminals by the government and by the public, including many who support their goals. A commitment to non-violence is the best respected of the principles defining what is an NGO.

Types of NGOs

Nongovernmental organizations are an heterogeneous group. A long list of acronyms has developed around the term 'NGO'.

These include:

- INGO stands for international NGO, such as CARE, Helvetas (Swiss Association for International Cooperation), RESPECT Refugiados, International Alert, ADFA-India ZOA Refugee Care, Medair and Mercy Corps;
- BINGO is short for business-oriented international NGO;
- RINGO is an abbreviation of religious international

NGO such as Catholic Relief Services or stands for Research and Independent Non-governmental organization;

- ENGO, short for environmental NGO, such as Global 2000;
- GONGOs are government-operated NGOs, which may have been set up by governments to look like NGOs in order to qualify for outside aid or promote the interests of the government in question;
- QUANGOs are quasi-autonomous non-governmental organisations, such as the W3C and the International Organization for Standardization (ISO), which is actually not purely an NGO, since its membership is by nation, and each nation is represented by what the ISO Council determines to be the 'most broadly representative' standardization body of a nation. Now, such a body might in fact be a nongovernmental organization—for example, the United States is represented in ISO by the American National Standards Institute, which is independent of the federal government. However, other countries can be represented by national governmental agencies—this is the trend in Europe.

There are also numerous classifications of NGOs. The typology the World Bank uses divides them into Operational and Advocacy:

The primary purpose of an operational NGO is the design and implementation of development-related projects. One categorization that is frequently used is the division into 'relief-oriented' or 'development-oriented' organizations; they can also be classified according to whether they stress service delivery or participation; or whether they are religious and secular; and whether they are more public or private-oriented. Operational NGOs can be community-based, national or international.

The primary purpose of an Advocacy NGO is to defend or promote a specific cause. As opposed to operational project management, these organizations typically try to raise awareness, acceptance and knowledge by lobbying, press work and activist events.

The primary purpose of an operational NGO is the design and implementation of development-related projects. One categorization that is frequently used is the division into 'relief-oriented' or 'development-oriented' organizations; they can also be classified according to whether they stress service delivery or participation; or whether they are religious and secular; and whether they are more public or private-oriented. Operational NGOs can be community-based, national or international.

The primary purpose of an Advocacy NGO is to defend or promote a specific cause. As opposed to operational project management, these organizations typically try to raise awareness, acceptance and knowledge by lobbying, press work and activist events.

There is a great variety of ways in which NGOs are structured. The classic model is of a membership organization, co-ordinated in a geographically-defined hierarchy. Individual people work in local groups, which co-ordinate in provinces and then have a headquarters in the capital city for the country as a whole. Such country-wide organizations are called national NGOs. Frequently, the national NGOs combine in an international NGO, or INGO, which may consist of regional groups of countries and be capped by a global body. Not all the levels of the hierarchy need exist. Many countries are too small to have provincial structures. Smaller specialist NGOs may simply enroll individual members at the national level, without having any local branches. Occasionally, individuals are enrolled at the international level. On the other hand, in large organizations, the international level often seems relatively remote and attracts little attention, even among the NGO's own members. The group running a local family planning clinic does not necessarily know about the work of the International Planned Parenthood Federation (IPPF) at the UN World Conference on Women in Beijing. Nevertheless, such global organizations with their membership measured in millions do maintain a democratic policy-making process. While some may hold direct elections for key posts at the national level, the responsibility to the membership at the global level is always indirect, via some international council or assembly of national representatives.

It should be noted that one of the ambiguities about the term, NGO, is whether it is referring to a local, provincial, national, regional or global body. Until the early 1990s, the matter was generally straightforward in academic, news media or political discussions. The overwhelming majority of local and provincial NGOs never engaged in transnational activities. Thus NGO, by itself, usually meant a national NGO and regional or global bodies were called international NGOs. National NGOs did engage in transnational development and humanitarian activities, but, with very few exceptions, they were not, in their own right, participants in international diplomacy. When they wanted to exercise political influence at the global level, they did so through the appropriate INGO. In the 1990s, there was a great upsurge in local organizations becoming active at the global level, particularly on environmental issues, because of the Rio Earth Summit in June 1992, and on social issues, because of the Copenhagen Social Summit in March 1995. Since then, the term INGO has not been used so much and NGO, by itself, has come to cover both national and international NGOs. As an expression of the new politics, various terms then were popularized to refer to local NGOs. Grass-roots organizations, community based organizations (CBOs), and civil society organizations (CSOs), all came into currency. There is still an ambiguity whether these newer terms cover organizations that only operate at the local level or also include local branches of national organizations. Grass-roots and community organizations clearly refer solely to the local level, but civil society has connotations of any level within a single country. Indeed, it has become quite common to refer to global civil society.

Linguistic usage in the legal atmosphere at the UN used to be somewhat different. When the UN was formed, any involvement of private individuals or groups in its work constituted deviation from the norm of diplomacy being the exclusive preserve of "states". Thus, a national organization, as mentioned in Article 71 of the UN Charter, was any NGO based in a single country. No distinction was made between an organization that covered a large constituency, over the whole country, and an organization based solely in a local community or a small section of the population. The lack of any distinction did not matter, as participation by either country-wide or more limited national NGOs was so rare in the permanent UN organs. Participation began on a small scale in the 1970s at UN conferences, on an *ad hoc* basis. When the ECOSOC rules were changed in 1996, to admit "national NGOs" to consultative status as a matter of routine, the presumption became that a national organization was a country-wide membership organization or a federation of local groups or an umbrella group, that is a coalition of NGOs operating in different fields. As is common at the UN, practice has not been consistent: a few local NGOs have been admitted as "national NGOs" to consultative status. The Rio conference also produced a term that has only been used in environmental politics at the UN. "Major Groups" refers to a system of categorizing NGOs from all levels, for the purposes of participating in UN policy-making processes.

A minority of NGOs conform to the model of a global democratic hierarchy, in which any person may become a member. One variant is for the NGO to have subscribers or supporters, providing income, receiving newsletters and responding to calls for action, but not having any democratic control either over expenditure or over policy priorities for the organization. This is common among altruistic NGOs, promoting social welfare and poverty alleviation, and also among environmental NGOs. Another variant is for a specific status or participation in some activity to be a prerequisite for membership. Thus trade unions are only open to those employed in certain occupations (sometimes very broadly defined). Similarly, professional, scientific and technical bodies are only open to people with the relevant qualification. Such organizations may then be grouped on a functional basis rather than a geographical basis, before they form national and/or international federations. Trade unions do maintain democratic decision-making structures (at least in principle, if not always in practice). However, professional, scientific and technical bodies have professional norms that override democratic norms and members may be expelled for violating the professional norms. A third variant is a religious organization. The major religions do all have complex hierarchies, from the local faith community through to global spiritual authorities. None of them claim to be democratic: authority is based on faith, a holy text, the charisma of individuals or a hierarchical tradition. To some it will be surprising to discuss trade unions, professional bodies and religious organizations as if they are NGOs. Indeed, the leaders of all three will usually deny they are NGOs. Nevertheless, they are treated on the same basis as NGOs throughout the UN system, with the exception of the special place for unions in the International Labour Organisation's tripartite system of governance.

Public Relations

Non-governmental organizations need healthy relationships with the public to meet their goals. Foundations and charities use sophisticated public relations campaigns to raise funds and employ standard lobbying techniques with governments. Interest groups may be of political importance because of their ability to influence social and political outcomes. At times NGOs seek to mobilize public support.

Consulting

Many international NGOs have a consultative status with United Nations agencies relevant to their area of work. As an example, the Third World Network has a consultative status with the UN Conference on Trade and Development (UNCTAD) and the UN Economic and Social Council (ECOSOC). While in 1946, only 41 NGOs had consultative status with the ECOSOC, by 2003 this number had risen to 2,350.

Project Management

There is an increasing awareness that management techniques are crucial to project success in non-governmental organizations. Generally, non-governmental organisations, which are private, have a community or environmental focus. They address varieties of issues such as religion, emergency aid, and humanitarian affairs. They mobilize public support and voluntary contributions for aid; they often have strong links with community groups in developing countries and they often work in areas where government-to-government aid is not possible. NGO's are accepted as a part of the international relations landscape, and while they influence national and multilateral policy-making, they are, increasingly, more directly involved in local action.

Management of NGOs

Two management trends are particularly relevant to NGOs: diversity management and participatory management. Diversity management deals with different cultures in an organization. Intercultural problems are prevalent in Northern NGOs that are engaged in developmental activities in the South. Personnel coming from a rich country are faced with a completely different approach of doing things in the target country. A participatory management style is said to be typical of NGOs. It is intricately tied to the concept of a learning organization: all people within the organization are perceived as sources for knowledge and skills. To develop the organization, individuals have to be able to contribute in the decision making process and they need to learn.

Staffing

Not all people working for non-governmental organizations are volunteers. Paid staff members typically receive lower pay than in the commercial private sector. Employees are highly committed to the aims and principles of the organization. The reasons why people volunteer are not necessarily purely altruistic, and can provide immediate benefits for themselves as well as those they serve, including skills, experience and contacts.

There is some dispute as to whether expatriates should be sent to developing countries. Frequently this type of personnel is employed to satisfy a donor, who wants to see the supported project managed by someone from an industrialized country. However, the expertise these employees or volunteers may have can be counterbalanced by a number of factors: the cost of foreigners is typically higher, they have no grassroot connections in the country they are sent to and local expertise is often undervalued.

The NGO-sector is an important employer in terms of numbers. For example, by the end of 1995, CONCERN worldwide, an international Northern NGO working against poverty, employed 174 expatriates and just over 5,000 national staff working in ten developing countries in Africa and Asia, and in Haiti.

Coalition-Building Among NGOs

Once NGOs do decide to influence public policy, they organize, in broad coalitions, specifically for this purpose. This means there is a large number of NGOs that bear no resemblance to the classic model of a unified hierarchy. Coalitions may take the form of umbrella INGOs, networks or caucuses. In the days when the main form of communication was by mail and even transnational telephone conversations were expensive and time-consuming to arrange, multi-national coalitions generally took the form of institutional structures. Many international women's organizations, the International Council of Voluntary Agencies and the World Conservation Union are examples that date from this era. They are referred to as umbrella organizations, to signify the presence under the single umbrella of a variety of different NGOs that do not share a common identity. In the 1960s, direct transnational telephone dialing was established and air travel became sufficiently cheap for individuals to meet occasionally. Then in the 1970s the news media gradually used satellite communications, so that events in one place were shared around the world as television images. These processes encouraged the formation of looser issue-based networks of NGOs to exchange information, mobilize support and co-ordinate strategies. At this stage, networks still required some degree of formal organization, with enough resources being raised to pay the salary of a network administrator and associated costs for the paperwork. The International Baby Foods Action Network was the prototype, followed by similar networks on pesticides, rainforests, climate change and other questions. The advent of e-mail and the web in the 1990s then meant that the costs of running a network dropped substantially and individual people could afford to take part in sophisticated instantaneous global communications. The number of networks increased dramatically and they no longer needed any formal structure. Once a lead organization or even a lead individual establishes technical and political communication skills, a coalition of thousands of NGOs can be formed rapidly and their influence focused on specific targets. The International Campaign to Ban Landmines, the Coalition for an International Criminal Court and Jubilee 2000 are the most spectacular examples. However, the impact of technological change should not be exaggerated. The most effective modern networks still derive their impact from being coalitions of well-organized NGOs. Although communication costs are now minimal, it is still essential to have sufficient resources at the center, even if they are provided by a single member of the network, for at least one person to devote most or all of his/her time to servicing the network.

A variant of the global network is a global caucus. This arises when a group of NGOs come together as lobbyists at an international diplomatic event, such as a UN agenda-setting conference or a UN forum for negotiating on the formulation or implementation of a treaty. The caucus will be highly focused on achieving specific outcomes from the diplomatic process. The impression is given that such a caucus is an ad hoc grouping that only exists during the two or three weeks of the relevant diplomatic meetings. It may be accurate that the particular combination of NGOs having the particular political purpose will never meet again. However, a successful caucus will be well prepared and will carry forward procedural expertise, substantive knowledge, political status and diplomatic contacts gained in one forum through to the next forum, handling similar questions. Key organizations and key individuals provide continuity. Women's organizations and environmentalists are among the most successful operating in this way.

When we consider something as loose and transient as a caucus, it is perhaps inappropriate to call it an organization. Nevertheless, structured umbrella coalitions, networks and caucuses are all handled in the same way by governments. In the UN system, all transnational actors have to accept the label "NGO", in order to participate. They may be present under the label of the coalition or of its constituents or through both routes. Umbrella INGOs have consultative status and networks usually are listed, but caucuses rarely have any formal recognition. Coalitions that focus on policy outcomes in a particular country or a particular intergovernmental organization will tend to take the form of an umbrella organization. Coalitions that focus on issues tend to take the form of a network or a caucus, with different members being active in different policy forums.

In global environmental politics, there is a unique set of caucuses – the system of "Major Groups". The term was adopted at the Earth Summit, when *Agenda 21* devoted one of its four sections to "Strengthening the Role of Major Groups". The preamble argued that "one of the fundamental prerequisites for the achievement of sustainable development is broad public participation in decision-making" and this must be done as a "real social partnership" with "individuals, groups and organizations". The aim was for the UN to move beyond the traditional reliance on the established NGOs, in two ways. Communication must reach down to individuals at the level of local communities and particular sectors of society of importance for the environment must be mobilized. The section devoted separate chapters to nine Major Groups, under the following headings.

- Global action for women towards sustainable and equitable development
- Children and youth in sustainable development
- Recognising and strengthening the role of indigenous people and their communities
- Strengthening the role of non-governmental organizations: partners for sustainable development
- Local authorities' initiatives in support of *Agenda 21*
- Strengthening the role of workers and their trade unions
- Strengthening the role of business and industry
- Scientific and technological community
- Strengthening the role of farmers.

The choice of these nine groups was the arbitrary and incoherent outcome of negotiations at UNCED. It was influenced by the personal concerns of Maurice Strong and by the lobbying of NGOs who were accredited to the conference. It is arbitrary to single out women but not men; the young but not the elderly; indigenous people but not other minorities; unions but not professional associations; business and industry but not commerce, finance and services; natural scientists but not social scientists; and farmers but not fishing communities. It is anomalous, but understandable, to emphasize one level of government, local authorities, when they have responsibility for all the Major Groups. Above all it is incoherent to have NGOs as one of the Major Groups, when *all* the other eight (including associations of local authorities) are represented in the UN system via the ECOSOC "arrangements for consultation with non-governmental organizations". This incoherence arises because many in the other Major Groups did not wish to be labeled as NGOs and there had to be a category to encompass environment and development NGOs.

In the Commission on Sustainable Development set up after the Earth Summit, special arrangements were made to allow for participation by all the new groups that had engaged with the UN for the first time at Rio. Any NGO that had been accredited for UNCED was allowed to apply for Roster NGO status at sessions of the CSD and later was given a special fast-track procedure for gaining full status with ECOSOC. Although the CSD is constitutionally a standard subsidiary body of ECOSOC, it has developed its own procedures for relating to NGOs. Rather than each NGO attempting to exercise its participation rights separately, the NGOs are organized into the nine Major Groups from *Agenda 21*. These categories are used both by the NGOs in their own caucusing and in the formal proceedings. In addition, the CSD has gone beyond the normal consultative arrangements to hold various types of formal, and informal, panels and seminars. Notably, each of the annual sessions starts with the appropriate Major Groups making presentations in special "stakeholder dialogues" on the different substantive agenda items for that year. In pragmatic terms, the illogicality of having NGOs as one of the nine groups of NGOs serves a useful function, in enabling any organization that does not fit elsewhere to be included. This Major Groups system has only operated in the CSD and in other processes that have been derived from UNCED.

The Geographical Spread of NGOs

It used to be widely argued that NGOs were predominantly a feature of Western societies. This false proposition was derived from a mixture of ignorance, Western presumptions of their superiority in the Cold War and nationalist rhetoric from authoritarian regimes. All societies in modern times have had large numbers of NGOs at least at the local level. Under the most authoritarian regimes or in the least developed countries there are still self-help co-operative groups, community welfare associations, religious groups, professional and scientific associations, sports and recreational bodies, etc. Even Romania during the dictatorship of President Ceaucescu was host to the International Federation of Beekeepers' Associations. The presence or absence of a democratic political culture is one of the major variables determining the number of NGOs, but the size of a country, its ethnic, religious and cultural diversity, the complexity of its economy and the quality of its communication infrastructure are also of crucial importance. Thus there are tens of thousands of NGOs in countries such as Bangladesh and India, while there are relatively few in Iceland or Finland.

A particular source of controversy is the idea that the major NGOs are "Northern". Many people are still trapped by the mental prejudice that organizations have to be situated in geographical space. It might be a practical necessity for an international NGO to have a headquarters office in a particular building, but the location of the office in a North American or a European city does not convert a global NGO into a Northern NGO. Equally, the historical origins of an organization being formed in a particular country does not mean it is currently a Northern rather than a global organization. The proper criteria for assessment whether an organization is global are the location of its membership, the staffing of its headquarters, the sources of its funding and the content of its programs. An organization, such as Amnesty International, with 56 National Sections, groups in some 40 other countries, an International Secretariat from over 50 countries and an African Secretary-General is a global NGO, even if it started in Britain and has its headquarters in London. Due to the spread of democracy and the improvements in communications, many international NGOs that started in individual countries became global at the end of the twentieth century.

Types of NGO Activities

Much as observers wish to gain greater understanding by defining different categories of NGOs, it is not possible to do so. We may distinguish different activities, but specific NGOs will often change the balance of the activities they pursue. The most common distinction is between operational and campaigning NGOs. This may be interpreted as the choice between small-scale change achieved directly through projects and large-scale change promoted indirectly through influence on the political system.

Operational NGOs have to mobilize resources, in the form of financial donations, materials or volunteer labor, in order to sustain their projects and programs. This process may require quite complex organization. Charity shops, staffed by volunteers, in premises provided at nominal rents and selling donated goods, end up providing finance to the national headquarters. Students in their vacations or during a break in their education provide labor for projects. Finance obtained from grants or contracts, from governments, foundations or companies, require time and expertise spent on planning, preparing applications, budgeting, accounting and reporting. Major fund-raising events require skills in advertising, media relations and motivating supporters. Thus, operational NGOs need to possess an efficient headquarters bureaucracy, in addition to the operational staff in the field. Campaigning NGOs will carry out much the same functions, but with a different balance between them. Fund-raising is still necessary, but on a smaller scale and it can serve the symbolic function of strengthening the donors' identification with the cause. Persuading people to donate their time is necessary, but, in addition to a small number of people giving a great deal of time, it is also necessary to be able to mobilize large numbers for brief periods. External donors may not impose onerous administrative burdens, but supporters still have to be supplied with information on an efficient regular basis. Major events will aim to attract favorable publicity rather than raise funds.

Therefore, despite their differences, both operational and campaigning NGOs need to engage in fund-raising, mobilization of work by supporters, organizing special events, cultivating the media and administering a headquarters. Only the defining activities – implementing projects or holding demonstrations – serve to differentiate them. In reality, the distinctions are not as sharp as the labels suggest. Operational NGOs often move into campaigning when projects regularly face similar problems and the impact of the projects seems to be insufficient. All the large development and environment operational NGOs now run some regular campaigns, at least by supporting campaigning networks. Similarly, campaigning NGOs often feel they cannot ignore the immediate practical problems of people in their policy domain. Human rights NGOs and women's NGOs end up having programs to assist the victims of discrimination and injustice.

Various other types of NGOs can be regarded as promoting change by variants on these two primary functions. Research institutes have special forms of operational programs, in which the goal is to increase knowledge and understanding. They range across a spectrum from those promoting an academic, non-political image to those collating and disseminating information for campaigning purposes. Professional bodies, trade unions, recreational groups and associations of companies provide program activities required by and for their members, but they may also campaign to enhance the economic interests and the status of their organizations. These categories and several others have some practical value for everyday discourse, but they do not provide the basis for an analytical classification of NGOs.

The most effective way to distinguish between NGOs is to obtain precise data on a range of different variables. The number of full-time employees, the number of members and the funding of the annual budget give measures of the size of any NGO. Opinion poll data on recognition of and support for an NGO or its goals, along with the frequency of positive mentions in the news media, give measures of its political strength. There are also more subjective variables, such as the professional skill, knowledge and experience of the personnel, that matter for both operational and campaigning purposes.

NGOs, Social Movements and Civil Society

Among some political activists, there is a tendency to see organizations, particularly hierarchical organizations, as conservative and oppressive. As a result NGOs may be seen as part of the established order. This view is enhanced by the fact that prominent NGOs may have a long history, complex structures, technical literature and a leadership who engage more with global politics than with their members or supporters. Thus at times NGOs are contrasted with the 'new social movements'. These can be portrayed as dynamic, innovative and non-hierarchical.

The idea of a movement simultaneously invokes two dissimilar ideas: the political impact of mass action, by very large numbers of people, and the role of the individual person, independently making his/her own voice heard. The oldest example is the labor movement, going back to the nineteenth century. Since the 1960s, there have been references to the new social movements, such as those for peace, women's rights, development, the environment and anti-racism. They were 'new', partly because they were not based on class divisions and partly because new methods of mass mobilization became possible. In December 1999, a higher level of aggregation, into a diffuse and incoherent coalition, was recognized as the anti-globalization movement, when mass demonstrations disrupted the Seattle Ministerial

Conference of the World Trade Organization.

In practice, the conservative/radical contrast between NGOs and social movements cannot be sustained. There are both conservative and radical NGOs and many other shades of political opinion along the spectrum. There are some writers, including some academics, who refer to 'progressive' social movements, as if all social movements were progressive. This ignores the existence of reactionary social movements, such as neo-fascists and racists, who cannot be distinguished from other movements by any objective criteria.

This must be kept in mind that NGOs should not be contrasted with social movements, because NGOs are *essential* components of social movements. If an idea is to catch the imagination of people, it has to be articulated by leaders through speeches, pamphlets or visual images. If the idea is going to reach large numbers of people, resources have to be mobilized and allocated to communication processes. If demonstrations are to occur, they have to be organized. If a movement is to achieve change, priorities have to be selected and targets designated. If a protest lasts more than a few days to become a movement, existing organizations or new organizations will provide the skeleton that transforms an amorphous mass into a strong body. This is not to say that social movements are composed solely of NGOs.

A social movement consists of a range of organizations who collaborate for some common purpose that is sufficiently compelling to generate a sense of collective identity, *along with* all the people, within and outside the organizations, who identify with the common goals and the collective identity. Thus, a social movement is more than a coalition of NGOs and less than society as a whole. In the 1990s, four mutually-reinforcing processes of change led to emphasis on the concept of civil society. There was an explosion in global communication facilities; the new forms of private association, from transnational community organizations to networks and caucuses, were recognized; the fall of communist regimes in Eastern Europe and military regimes in developing countries promoted participation in the new democratic systems; and the major UN conferences produced an unprecedented scale of global public engagement with intergovernmental events. In addition, the secretariats of the UN and other intergovernmental organizations sought to overcome the crises generated by the unilateralism of United States administrations and the failure of Congress to deliver US financial obligations, by appealing to global civil society as a source of legitimacy for international co-operation.

In simple words "civil society" is all public activity, by any individuals, organizations or movements, other than government employees acting in a governmental capacity. In the broadest sense, it encompasses all social, economic, cultural and political relations, but the emphasis is usually on the political aspects of these relations. Thus, it can be used in reference to any level from the local to the country as a whole, or even global interactions. It also clearly goes beyond traditional NGOs to all forms of networks, caucuses and movements. As a result, it serves as a political tool for all those who want to promote innovative, wider and deeper levels of political participation. In contrast with the paucity of civil society activities in former authoritarian regimes, it is sometimes implied that civil society is in opposition to government. However, academics who adopt the "critical theory" approach of Habermas take the opposite view. They see civil society as integrated with the state in maintaining bourgeois hegemony in capitalist societies.

This approach is virtually unknown outside non-academic circles. A second confusion is whether civil society includes or excludes the economic activities. For some, civil society encompasses everything except government, but for others there are three quite separate realms: government, civil society and the economy. On the basis of the former assumption, the United Nations used the term civil society to express its desire to strengthen its relations with both companies and NGOs. The result was furious protests from those NGOs who blame companies for social exploitation, poverty and environmental degradation. Lastly, as with several other terms, some people wish to see civil society solely in a positive light and exclude actors of whom they disapprove. Not only criminals and drug dealers, but also "reactionary" NGOs, are occasionally referred to as "uncivil society". Despite these various problems, civil society is a useful way of going beyond the traditional NGOs and referring to all the ways in which diverse non-governmental actors are mobilized. Nevertheless, it is necessary to be explicit on whether economic actors are being included or not.

Summing Up

Generally it is assumed that all NGOs are politically active. This is obviously not the case, irrespective of the political situation or the issue under consideration. At any specific point in time, an NGO may have little contact with those who are not members. On the other hand, a change in society that is salient to the group can motivate an introspective NGO to engage in sustained political action. It is certainly not true that all NGOs are active in global politics. It is not even true that all NGOs attempt to influence politics at the country level, in the narrow sense of direct engagement in the debate over public policy.

However, politics may also be seen, more broadly, as the process by which any set of people reaches a collective decision. This means that attempts by an NGO to mobilize individuals and change their personal behavior, to win support from a religious group or a trade union, or to articulate their values in the news media are all forms of political action. Legal systems may classify raising money for purposes such as poverty alleviation, disaster relief or environmental conservation as non-political, but the legal distinction between charitable and political activity is always based on an arbitrary, illogical and controversial definition of politics. Many NGOs will not see themselves as engaging directly in public policy, but their activities are always a social expression of values. Hence, NGOs are very likely to be political in the broadest sense of affecting social discourse and can often have an indirect effect on politics in the narrow sense of shaping public policy.

The point of this debate about terminology is to emphasize that NGOs are not just well-meaning, uncontroversial, non-political groups. Furthermore, there is no difference between the role of NGOs in domestic and in global politics. At both levels, they are diverse, controversial and of major political significance. The impact of a particular NGO may vary across time and place, and from one issue to another, but collectively NGOs generate the dynamics of political change. We have seen that there is often an assumption that NGOs are operating for the general public good or even that they are "progressive". However, there is such diversity to the values advocated by different NGOs that they oppose each other, as well as putting pressure on governments and companies. Many women's NGOs oppose religious NGOs on questions of sexual and reproductive behavior. Hunters, farmers and fishing communities oppose animal rights groups.

Environmental and development NGOs have different perspectives on sustainable development from each other. Many radical NGOs are hostile to reformist NGOs who accept incremental change. It is not logically possible for anybody to support all NGOs nor indeed to be hostile to all NGOs.

Many government leaders express quite hostile attitudes to NGOs, even in some democratic societies. In as much as this is a general sentiment, it is irrational. There are particular factors that explain the irrationality. Firstly, the increased impact of NGOs has caused resentment among those whom they criticize. Secondly, the claim by some NGOs that they are the "voice of the people" and hence have greater legitimacy than governments is deeply offensive to government officials. As they are quick to point out, it is also a ludicrous claim. Thirdly, the violence and the extreme revolutionary and/or nihilistic attitudes associated with some of the participants in a series of anti-globalization demonstrations, starting at Seattle in 1999, diminished the status of the other NGOs at the demonstrations. In some circles, there was even a generalized negative impact upon NGOs from the terrorist attacks upon New York and Washington in September 2001. Nevertheless, virtually all government leaders, in both domestic and global politics, including those who have expressed hostility, will work with NGOs when they expect the most active NGOs to be allies, in support of their current political goals.

Denial of NGO's democratic legitimacy arises when democracy is simply reduced to the right to take part in governmental decision-making. Clearly, on this limited basis, NGOs cannot claim a greater legitimacy than elected governments. Many NGOs themselves do not have democratic procedures within their own organizations and many only represent a small number of people. Even the minority of NGOs that elect their leaders, have conferences to decide their policies and have millions of members, still have no basis to claim a right to take decisions on behalf of society as a whole. These arguments were obscured in the 1970s and 1980s when many NGOs significantly expanded their membership and their activities. In this period, more governments were authoritarian than democratic. Under regimes that are communist, feudal, fascist, military dictatorships or corrupt oligarchies it might be reasonable to claim NGOs are more representative of society as a whole, but such regimes have become the exception in a world of democracies from the 1990s onwards.

However, a wider view of democracy totally legitimizes the role of NGOs. Democracy is not just the holding of elections every four or five years. It is also the continuous process of debate, in which the legislature, the political parties, the media and society as a whole put questions on the political agenda, formulate alternative policy proposals and criticize the policy of the government. On this basis, any NGO has a right to participate, however large or small and however representative or unrepresentative of a particular sector of society it may be. Indeed, in both domestic and global politics, policy-making could not be democratic without the active participation of NGOs.

REFERENCES

A. Thomas, S. Carr and D. Humphreys (eds.) (2001), *Environmental Policies and NGO Influence. Land Degradation and Sustainable Resource Management in Sub-Saharan Africa*, (London: Routledge).

B. Arts, M. Noortmann and B. Reinalda (eds.) (2001), *Non-State Actors in International Relations*, (Aldershot: Ashgate).

C. Rootes (ed.) (1999), *Environmental Movements. Local, National and Global*, (London: Frank Cass).

Chiang Pei-heng (1981), *Non-Governmental Organizations at the United Nations. Identity, Role and Function*, (New York: Praeger).

D. Humphreys (1996), *Forest Politics. The Evolution of International Co-operation*, (London: Earthscan).

D. Josselin and W. Wallace (eds.) (2001), *Non-State Actors in World Politics*, (Houndmills: Palgrave).

Florini, Ann, ed. The Third Force: The Rise of Transnational Civil Society (Carnegie Endowment for International Peace and Japan Center for International Exchange, 2001).

Hall, Rodney Bruce and Biersteker, Thomas. The Emergence of Private Authority in Global Governance (Cambridge Studies in International Relations, 2003)

Hilhorst, Dorthea. The Real World of NGOs: Discourses, Diversity and Development, Zed Books, 2003

J. Fisher (1998, *Nongovernments. NGOs and the Political Development of the Third World*, West Hartford: Kumarian Press).

J. McCormick (1995), *The Global Environmental Movement*, (Chichester: John Wiley and Sons).

J. W. Foster with A. Anand (eds.) (1999), *Whose World is it Anyway? Civil Society, the United Nations and the Multilateral Future*, (Ottawa: United Nations Association in Canada).

M. Edwards and J. Gaventa (eds.) (2001), *Global Citizen Action*, (Boulder: Lynne Rienner).

M. K. Meyer and E. Prügel (eds.) (1999), *Gender Politics in Global Governance*, (Lanham: Rowman and Littlefield Publishers).

P. J. Nelson (1995), *The World Bank and Non-Governmental Organizations. The Limits of Apolitical Development*, (New York: St. Martin's Press and Houndmills: Macmillan Press).

P. Willetts (ed.) (1996), *'The Conscience of the World'. The Influence of Non-Governmental Organizations in the UN System*, (Washington: Brookings Institution and London: Christopher Hurst).

R. O'Brien, A. M. Goetz, J. A. Scholte and M. Williams (2000), *Contesting Global Governance. Multilateral Economic*

Institutions and Global Social Movements, (Cambridge: Cambridge University Press).

Rodman, K (1998)."'Think Globally, Punish Locally: Nonstate Actors, Multinational Corporations, and Human Rights Sanctions" in Ethics in International Affairs, vol. 12.

Roelofs, Joan. Foundations and Public Policy: The Mask of Pluralism (Albany: State University of New York Press, 2003).

Smillie, Ian, & Minear, Larry, editors. The Charity of Nations: Humanitarian Action in a Calculating World, Kumarian Press, 2004

T. G. Weiss and L. Gordenker (eds.) (1996), *NGOs, the UN and Global Governance*, (Boulder CO: Lynne Rienner).

T. Princen and M. Finger (1994), *Environmental NGOs in World Politics. Linking the Local and the Global*, (London: Routledge).

T. Risse-Kappen (ed.) (1995), *Bringing Transnational Relations Back In. Non-State Actors, Domestic Structures and International Institutions*, (Cambridge: Cambridge University Press).

Tarrow, Sydney. The New Transnational Activism, New York:Cambridge University Press, 2005

Teegen, H. Doh, J., Vachani, S., 2004. "The importance of nongovernmental organisation in global governance and value creation: an international business research agenda" in Journal of International Business Studies. Washington: Vol. 35, Iss.6.

Teegen, H., 2003. 'International NGOs as Global Institutions: Using Social Capital to Impact Multinational Enterprises and Governments', Journal of International Management.

Ward, Thomas, editor. Development, Social Justice, and Civil Society: An Introduction to the Political Economy of NGOs, Paragon House, 2005

2

NGO Formation: Procedure & Practices

I

A Non Governmental Organization (NGO) is perceived to be an association of persons or a body of individuals. An association of persons with non-profit motive may be registered under any of the following Indian Acts:

1. As a Charitable Trust
2. As a Society registered under the Societies Registration Act
3. As a Company licensed under section 25 of the Companies Act

Procedures

Trust: "Trust" is defined as an obligation annexed to the ownership of property, and arising out of a confidence reposed in and accepted by the owner or declared and accepted by him for the benefit of another, or of another and the owner.

A Trust may be created by any language sufficient to know the intention and no technical words are necessary. A trust deed, generally, incorporates the following:

i. The name(s) of the author(s)/settlor(s) of the trust;
ii. The name(s) of the trustee(s);

iii. The name(s) if any, of the beneficiary/ies or whether it shall be the public at large;

iv. The name by which the trust shall be known;

v. The name where its principal and/or other offices shall be situate;

vi. The property that shall devolve upon the trustee(s) under the trust for the benefit of the beneficiary/ies;

vii. An intention to divest the trust property upon the trustee(s);

viii. The objects of the trust;

ix. The procedure for appointment, removal or replacement of a trustee. Their rights, duties and powers etc;

x. The rights and duties of the beneficiary/ies;

xi. The mode and method of determination of the trust.

A charitable trust is not required to obtain registration under the Indian Registration Act.

Society

A society may be defined as a company or an association of persons united together by mutual consent to deliberate, determine and act jointly for same common purpose. Minimum seven persons, eligible to enter into a contract, can form society. When an NGO is constituted as a society, it is required to be registered under the Societies Registration Act, 1860.

The chief advantage of forming a society are that it gives a corporate appearance to the organization, and provides greater flexibility as it is easier to amend the memorandum and bye laws of the society than in case of trust, terms of which are strictly manifested in the trust deed. However, formation of a society requires more procedural formalities than in case of a trust.

A Society for its inception requires:-

I. Memorandum of Association, and
II. Rules and Regulations

For the purpose of registration, following documents are required to be filed with the registrar of Societies:

a) Covering letter requesting for registration stating in the body of the letter various documents annexed to it. The letter is to be signed by all the subscribers to the memorandum or by a person duly authorised by all of them to sign on their behalf.

b) Memorandum of Association, in duplicate neatly typed and pages serially numbered.

c) Rules and Regulations/Bye-Laws, in duplicate, certified by at least three members of the governing body.

d) An affidavit of the president/Secretary of the society, on a non-judicial stamp paper of prescribed value, stating the relationship between the subscribers, duly attested by an oath commissioner, notary public or 1st class magistrate.

e) Documentary proof such as house tax receipt, rent receipt in respect of premises shown as registered office of the society or no objection certificate from the landlord of the premises.

f) An authority duly signed by all members of the managing committee.

g) A declaration by the members of the managing committee that the funds of the society shall be used only for the purpose of furthering the aims and objects of the society.

Company

Under Section 25 of the company's act, an association formed or to be formed:

a) For the purposes of promoting commerce, art, science, religion, charity ot any other useful object
b) With intention to apply its profits or other income for promoting its objects, and
c) Which prohibits payment of any dividend to its members,

Is permitted to be incorporated without addition of the word "Limited" or "Private Limited". Procedure for applying is same as applicable in the case of all companies.

If the registrar is satisfied that all formalities have been complied with, he will issue a certificate of incorporation from which date the company comes into existence.

Note: An association already registered as a company, may also apply for a licence u/s 25.

Income Tax Exemption for NGO

Trust

Under section 11(1)(a) to (c), income derived from property held under trust is exempt if the following conditions are satisfied:a) The property should be held under trust wholly for charitable or religious purposes.b) Income from such property should be applied to charitable or religious purposes. (Exemption is available to the extent of such application)c) Income should be applied in Indiad) At least 85% of the income derived from property held under trust, should be applied to charitable or religious purposes in the relevant previous year in order to claim full tax exemption.Note: (1) The assessee is to apply for registration in Form No. 10A in duplicate before the expiry of 1 year from the creation of trust. (2) Under Section 11(4) property held under trust includes a business undertaking held under trust. (3) Any voluntary contribution received by a trust or institution is exempt if (a) the trust is created wholly for charitable purposes and (b) contribution is not made with a specific direction that it shall form part of the corpus of the trust.

Society

Societies are taxable in the status of AOP and different rates of tax are applicable to the income of an AOP in different circumstances:

A. Individual shares of members in AOP are not determinate:

i. Where the total income of any member of the AOP is taxable at a rate higher than the maximum marginal rate-Rate of tax is such higher rate.

ii. Otherwise-30%

B. Individual shares of members in AOP are determinate:

i. If total income of any member is not higher than Rs 50000/- (excluding share from AOP) and no member is taxable higher than 30%- Rate of tax on total income of AOP is the rate applicable to individuals.

ii. If total income of any member is higher than Rs 50000/- (excluding share from AOP) and no member is taxable higher than 30%- Rate of tax is 30%

iii. If any member is taxed higher than 30%, then (a) Tax on the portion of total income of AOP that is relatable to the share of such member is levied at such rate higher than the 30%, (b) tax on the balance total income will be 30%.

Tax Exemption for Notified Charitable Societies U/S 10(23c) (IV) and (V)

Any income of any institution established for charitable purposes is exempt. For getting exemption under these clauses, following requirement must be completed:

i. Making an application in Form No. 56

ii. Applying its income or accumulating it for application, wholly & exclusively to its objects;

iii. Notice of accumulation u/s 11(2) will have to be given to the assessing officer in Form No. 10

II

This section provides all necesary information about NGO formation fund raising etc. in the form of Questions-Answers This may help the concerned persons a lot to make a firm decision in marching ahead.

What is a non-profit Company?

A non-profit company is like any other Company. There is only one important difference. It is not supposed to make profits. In other words, it does not exist for commercial gain.

Is it relevant for voluntary work?

Non-profit company has been designed for voluntary work only. It provides all the advantages of a corporate form to a Development Organisation.

What are the advantages?

- There is one uniform law across the country for companies (Companies Act 1956). And this is a very robust law, protected by powerful commercial interests. So it is difficult for a state government to take over a company.
- The corporate form also protects you better from those whisper-quiet internal take-overs that happen in a Trust or a Society.
- Company form provides voting rights according to number of shares held. This feature allows you to increase membership without worrying about controlling votes.
- No one else will be able to register a non-profit company anywhere in India with the same name and objectives as yours.
- The company form is recognised across the world. It is more closely regulated and is more respected as a form of organisation.

Today India is looking wide-eyed at the world. Indian NGOs are testing international waters. In such a situation, the non-profit company may be the logical choice for voluntary work in the third millennium.

Going back to basics, what is a Company?

A Company is very much like a society. In fact, both are corporate forms of organisation. A company has members (commonly called 'shareholders'), a Governing Body (Board of Directors), Memorandum and Articles.

A Company is different from a firm. Many firms are casually called 'companies'. For example, 'Amit & Company' actually means a firm.

This firm may be a partnership firm or a proprietorship firm. A proprietorship firm is owned by one single person. In a partnership, there are several partners, who share profits.

A real Company will always have the word 'Limited' at the end of the name. Normally it is written as 'Ltd.'. This means that the liability of its members is limited.

Do we need to renew the registration after few years?

No. If you keep filing the annual returns etc., no renewal is ever required.

On the other hand, society registration has to be renewed every five years in U.P., and each year in West Bengal.

What about the Charity Commissioner?

All public Trusts and Societies in Maharashtra and Gujarat have to be registered with the Charity commissioner.

Apparently, this requirement does not apply to non-profit Companies.

Can a non-profit Company pay salary to its directors?

Yes. They can pay salary to any director or office bearer who is working actively in the company. This applies across the country, including states like Tamilnadu (where office bearers of society can not draw remuneration).

The catch is that if any of the director is also a member (shareholder), then approval of the Central Government is needed for paying any salary or fees to that director.

Can a non-profit Company get FCRA?

Yes. A non-profit company is treated in exactly the same way as a society, so far as FCRA is concerned.

Is it very difficult to register a non-profit company?

Yes and no. It is probably less difficult than registering a society in some states. The advantage of a company is that you escape the whims and fancies of the Registrar of Societies. But...

You fall into the clutches of Registrar of Companies (ROC). Only saving grace is that at the ROC everything works according to written rules. And your C.A.s know most of the rules.

The real problem is with getting a license under section 25. This is needed so you can drop the word 'limited'. The license is issued by one of the four Regional Directors and is fairly difficult to get.

Are there many formalities later on?

Some of the formalities have been waived for non-profit companies. Still, the formalities are more than a society. And, most important, the ROC is pretty good at enforcing these formalities.

Who should go for a non-profit Company?

People who want to do things differently but want a rock-solid organisation structure. These people would probably be based in a state capital. They would be willing to invest a little extra time in paper work and reading the rulebook.

They may possibly like to call themselves 'social entrepreneurs'. They would be thinking of unusual, untested strategies of working and raising funds. They would definitely be interested in taking their work across state boundaries. And they may also be tempted by what lies beyond India's borders.

If you choose the company form, do it after careful thought. A non-profit company is not for the novice or the faint-hearted!

Registration Realities

Registering a non-profit company by yourself can be very frustrating. There are rules within rules. It would be best if you can get a CA firm or a lawyer (who specialises in companies) to register the company for you. The broad procedure is outlined below:

Choosing a name

ROC is supposed to ensure that two different companies do not get the same name. Therefore, you have to apply for prior-approval of the name. You can suggest four names, using form # 1-A.

This may take a week or two. A fee of Rs.50 has to be paid [Order u/s 613 dated 22-Dec-62]. For commercial companies the fee is Rs.500.

Memorandum & Articles

You then need to get your memorandum and articles approved by the Regional Director and the ROC. Articles are similar to bylaws.

There are some standard requirements for inclusion in these. There are printers who specialise in this. It is cost-effective to ask the printer whether they have a standard type-set. On the other hand, it is also a good idea to go through the articles carefully. This will help protect your Company later on from undesirable elements.

The printers normally agree to give you 4-8 copies initially. The ROC invariably asks for some changes in the Memorandum and Articles. The printer will deliver another 100-200 copies later after making these corrections or changes .

License under section 25

You have to apply to the Regional Director (Department of Company Affairs) for the above license. This license allows you to drop the word 'Limited' or 'Private Limited' from your name. The fee for this application is only Rs.60. There are four Regional Directors, at Mumbai, Calcutta, Chennai and Kanpur.

You will also have to publish a small notice about your application in two newspapers (English and a regional language).

The Regional Director may ask for reports from the District Magistrate, ROC and the State Government. However, in normal cases, ROC's report is sufficient.

Some follow-up and a visit to Regional Director may be required for getting this license. This process may take up to 4-5 months.

Registration with ROC

Make the corrections suggested by the Regional Director and ROC in the Memorandum and Articles. File these, along with section 25 license and other papers, at the ROC office in your state.

The registration procedure varies a little from state to state. However, the registration certificate is normally granted within one month after filing section 25 license.

No stamp duty is required for filing Memorandum and Articles. But you will have to pay registration fees. This depends on your share capital. If your authorised share capital is less than Rs.20,000 then total registration and filing fees will come to about Rs.500. If the capital is five lacs, then the fees will be around Rs.6,000. If you do not have a share capital, this may range from about Rs.200 to Rs.1,700.

ROC Offices

Office of the ROC is in the state capital in all states except the following:

- At Shillong for Assam, Tripura, Manipur, Nagaland, Arunachal, Mizoram.
- At Delhi for Haryana
- At Ahmedabad for Dadra and Nagar Haveli
- At Gwalior for Madhya Pradesh
- At Cuttack for Orissa
- At Jullundhur for Punjab, Himachal and Chandigarh
- At Kanpur for UP
- At Cochin for Kerala and for Lakshadweep, Minicoy, Amindivi Islands
- Additional office in Tamilnadu at Coimbatore for Districts of Coimbatore, Nilgiri, Periyar and Dharampuri

Costs of Registration

Total costs of registering a non-profit company may

range between Rs.8,000 to Rs.20,000. The figure includes all costs: ROC fees, printing, fees to CA / lawyer, advertisement and travel to Regional Director's office.

The total cost depends upon your share capital, fees of the CA or lawyer, and whether you have to travel to Regional Director's office.

Converting to Company

You can also convert your existing Society to a company. The procedure for this is broadly similar to above.

This may, however, require that you re-apply to FCRA for change in your FC registration.

Ambling Along

After you are registered, you can start or carry on your work in the normal manner. Just keep the following in mind:

Board Meetings

A Company works through its Board of Directors. This is similar to a society, which works through the managing committee or Governing Body.

Board meetings must be held regularly, normally once each quarter. Proper minutes should be maintained.

Annual General Meetings

The shareholders or members of a company must meet each year. At these meetings, they review annual accounts, elect some of the Directors and also appoint the auditors.

It is compulsory for companies to give copies of audited accounts to members.

Proper notice and minutes of these meetings are required.

Members in a company enjoy much more real power than in a Society. Their rights are also better protected by the Law. A member who can not attend personally can also vote by proxy. Members in a Company can not be removed so easily as in a society.

Auditors

Auditors are selected by the Board of Directors but appointed by the members. They also report to members.

Auditors of a society can be removed very easily. Removal is much more difficult in case of a company. This helps ensure independence of auditors.

Annual Returns

If there is any change in directors or office address, the ROC has to be informed. The audited accounts, annual report and an annual return have to be filed compulsorily with the ROC. Some important resolutions also have to be filed.

These requirements are enforced pretty strictly.

Annual Costs

The annual costs of running a company are not much more than in a society from the legal point of view. Only additional costs are for filing fees of documents, which averages between Rs.100 to Rs.500 each year.

But there are additional costs to be paid to C.A.s or lawyers for their advice and help with paper work. These may average around Rs.5,000 to Rs.15,000 each year.

Daring Disclosures

The key strength of a Company lies in its disclosure requirements. This improves transparency and increases public trust.

Conflict of Interest

All directors and important shareholders have to disclose names of their relatives each year. They also have to give names of other companies or concerns in which they are directors or shareholders.

They can not vote on any contract in which they may be interested. All such contracts are entered in a register.

Disclosure of Payments

If directors borrow money from the company, this has to be disclosed in the Balance Sheet. If the account has been settled within the year itself, still disclosure of maximum amount due is required.

Any other payment to the directors, their relatives, or their firms, has to be disclosed. Similarly, payments to highly paid employees have to be disclosed. All payments to auditors have to be disclosed.

Public Access

Members of the public can get copies of audited accounts, annual report, Memorandum etc. from the ROC. However, some portions of a private non-profit Company's accounts are not open to public.

Audited accounts of a society are also open to public in the same manner. However, in practise, locating accounts of a Society in the Registrar's office is very difficult.

Facts and Figures - How many?

How many non-profit companies are registered in India? The Registrar of Companies does not have clear statistics on this.

By 31st March '99, a total of 5,10,954 companies had been registered. We do not know how many of these were exempted under section 25. However, we know that at least 17,942 companies of these are classified under 'Community Social Services'.

Information Courtesy : Accountaid.net Visit Accountaid.net for the latest information.

What is Foreign Contribution ?

Foreign contribution means the donation, delivery or transfer, made by any foreign source of any,

a) article, not given to a person as a gift for personal use, if the market value, in India, of such article exceeds one thousand rupees;

b) currency, whether Indian or foreign; or,

c) foreign security

What is a Coreign Source ?

Foreign source includes the government of any foreign country or territory or its agency; an international agency; a foreign company; and citizen of a foreign country. Agencies of the United Nations, World Bank and some other International agencies/multilateral organisations are exempted from the definition of 'foreign source'.

List of such exempted agencies/organisations is available on the website *http://mha.nic.in/fore.htm*

Whether donation given by Non-Resident Indians (NRIs) is treated as 'foreign contribution'?

Contributions made by a citizen of India living in another country (i.e. Non-Resident Indian), from his personal savings, through the normal banking channels, is not treated as foreign contribution. However, while accepting any donations from such NRI, it is advisable to obtain his passport details to ascertain that he/she is an Indian passport holder.

Whether donations by Persons of Indian Origin (PIO) Card holder or Persons of Indian Origin (PIO) who hold other country's passports or registered Overseas Citizens of India (OCI) would be considered 'foreign source'?

Yes, because persons under all these three categories are foreign nationals and hold passports of the country of their nationality.

Whether foreigners can be appointed as Executive Committee members?

Foreign nationals are generally discouraged from being appointed as member of Executive Committee by an association. However, Foreign nationals, fulfilling the following conditions, may be appointed as Executive Committee members, after obtaining prior permission of the Central Government:

(i) the foreigner is married to an Indian citizen;

(ii) the foreigner has been living and working in India for at least five years;

(iii) the foreigner has made available his/her specialised knowledge, especially in the medical and health related fields on a voluntary basis in India, in the past;

(iv) the foreigner is part of the Board of Trustees/ Executive Committee in terms of the provisions in an inter-governmental agreement;

(v) the foreigner is part of the Board of Trustee/ Executive Committee, in an ex-officio capacity representing a multilateral body which is exempted from the definition of foreign source. The need for such an appointment should, however, be adequately justified.

Who can receive foreign contribution ?

An association having a definite cultural, economic, educational, religious or social programme can receive foreign contribution after it obtains the prior permission of the Central Government, or gets itself registered with the Central Government. An illustrative but not exhaustive list of activities which are permissible and may be carried out by associations of different nature are available on the website *http://mha.nic.in/fore.htm*

Who cannot receive foreign contribution ?

Foreign contribution cannot be accepted by:

(i) a candidate for election;

(ii) correspondent, columnist, cartoonist, editor, owner, printer or publisher of a registered newspaper;

(iii) judge, government servant or employee of any Corporation;

(iv) member of any legislature;

(v) political party or office bearer thereof; and

(vi) individuals or associations specifically notified under section 10 (a) of Foreign Contribution (Regulation) Act, 1976 who have been prohibited from receiving foreign contribution.

Can foreign contribution be received in and utilised from multiple Bank Accounts ?

No. All foreign contribution should be received in and utilised from same single Bank Account mentioned in the order for registration or prior permission granted by MHA. This account number is same as has been intimated by the organisation in their application for registration/prior permission. Use of multiple bank accounts is legally prohibited.

Can foreign contribution be mixed with local receipts?

No. Foreign contribution should not be mixed with local funds being handled by the organisation.

Can foreign contribution be received in rupees ?

Yes. Any amount received from 'foreign source' in rupees or foreign currency is construed as 'foreign contribution' under law. Such transactions even in rupees term is considered foreign contribution.

Will interest earned from foreign contribution be considered foreign contribution ?

Yes.

What is the Procedure for change of designated Bank Account ?

For change of the bank account, an application in prescribed form mentioning the details of the old bank account and the proposed new bank account alongwith justification for change may be submitted to MHA alongwith copy of resolution of the executive committee for such change. This form is available on website *http://mha.nic.in/fore.htm*. The new account may be made operational only after seeking MHA's approval.

What are the eligibility criteria for registration ?

An organisation in formative stage is not eligible for registration. Such organisation may apply for grant of prior permission under the law. For grant of registration, the association should:

(i) be registered under the Societies Registration Act, 1860 or the Indian Trusts Act, 1882 or section 25 of the Companies Act, 1956;

(ii) be in existence for at least three years and have made significant contribution in chosen area of activity. For this purpose, the association should have spent at least Rs.6,00,000 over last three years on its activities, excluding administrative expenditure. Statement of Income & Expenditure duly audited by Chartered Accountant for last three years may be enclosed to substantiate financial parameter.

What are the eligibility criteria for grant of prior permission ?

Prior permission is granted for receipt of specific amount from specific donor for carrying out specific activities/projects. For this purpose, the association should:

(i) be registered under the Societies Registration Act, 1860 or the Indian Trusts Act, 1882 or section 25 of the Companies Act, 1956;

(ii) submit commitment letter from the donor; and

(iii) submit copy of project for which foreign contribution is solicited/is being offered.

Whether recommendation of District Collector, etc., is mandatory ?

No. Submission of verification certificate from the District Collector, etc. is not mandatory. However, in certain cases, if the area of activity of an association is in non-border/coastal/tribal region and amount applied for prior permission is less than Rs.50 lakhs, submission of such a certificate assists in speedy clearance of the application.

What are the documents to be enclosed with the application ?

(a) Following documents should be enclosed with the application for grant of registration:

(i) Certified copy of registration certificate or Trust deed, as the case may be;

(ii) Details of activities during the last three years;

(iii) Copies of audited statement of accounts for the past three years (Asset and Liabilities, Receipt and Payment, Income and Expenditure);

(iv) If functioning as editor, owner, printer or publisher of a publication registered under the Press and Registration of Books Act, 1867, a certificate from the Press Registrar that the publication is not a newspaper in terms of section 1(1) of the said Act.

(b) Following documents should be enclosed with the application for grant of Prior Permission:

(i) Certified copy of registration certificate or Trust deed, as the case may be;

(ii) Commitment letter from foreign donor specifying the amount of foreign contribution;

(iii) Copy of project for which foreign contribution was solicited/is being offered;

(iv) If functioning as editor, owner, printer or publisher of a publication registered under the Press and Registration of Books Act, 1867, a certificate from the Press Registrar that the publication is not a newspaper in terms of section 1(1) of the said Act.

How to find the status of pending application for registration/prior permission. ?

Status of pending applications for grant of registration or prior permission may be checked on-line from the Ministry of Home Affairs' web-site – http://mha.nic.in/fore.htm. One needs to fill in the numbers on acknowledgement letter or any correspondence from MHA (Foreigners' Division) in the blank format which pops up on the screen after selection of status enquiry icon (registration/prior permission, as the case may be)

Is there any restrictions on transfer of funds to other organisations ?

Yes. No foreign contribution can be transferred from an association granted registration or prior permission under FCRA to another association unless the latter has also obtained either registration or prior permission under FCRA.

What is the procedure to be followed by a Liaison Office to receive foreign contribution.?

Prior permission under FCRA is required by a Liaison

Office of a foreign company for receiving remittances from its Head Office abroad for conducting conferences or carrying out other activities/programmes, etc. in India.

What is the procedure for filing of FC-3 returns ?

An association permitted to accept foreign contribution is required under law to maintain separate set of accounts and records exclusively for the foreign contribution received and utilised and submit an annual return, duly certified by a Chartered Accountant, giving details of the receipt and purpose-wise utilisation of the foreign contribution. The return is to be filed for every financial year (1st April to 31st March) within a period of four months from the closure of the year i.e. by 31st July of each year. Submission of even a 'Nil' return if there is no receipt/utilization of foreign contribution during the year, is mandatory, under law.

The return is to be submitted, in prescribed Form FC – 3, duly accompanied with the balance sheet and statement of receipt and payment, which is certified by a Chartered Accountant. The form is available on MHA's web-site – http://mha.nic.in/fore.htm.

What is foreign hospitality ?

Foreign Hospitality means any offer, not being a purely casual one, made by a foreign source for providing a person with the cost of travel to any foreign country or territory or with free board, lodging, transport or medical treatment.

Who cannot accept foreign hospitality without prior approval of MHA ?

No member of a legislature, office bearer of a political party, Judge, Government servant or employee of any corporation shall, while visiting any country or territory outside India, accept, except with the prior permission of the Central Government any foreign hospitality.

How one can seek permission of the Government for receiving foreign hospitality ?

Application form (form FC-2) for his purpose is available on MHA's web-site – http://mha.nic.in/fore.htm. One must apply on this form through the controlling officer at least three weeks in advance to seek prior approval of the Government for receiving foreign hospitality

Where should the applications be sent ?

All applications be sent to the Secretary, Ministry of Home Affairs, Foreigners' Division, Jaisalmer House, 26, Man Singh Road, New Delhi – 110011. The forms can be downloaded from the website *http://mha.nic.in/fore.htm.*

What is the procedure for seeking change in the name/address of the association ?

For seeking change in the name/address of the association, one should use the prescribed form available on MHA's website *http://mha.nic.in/fore.htm*

Who should be contacted for any information on FCRA ?

Names of the officers, their contact details including telephone numbers are available on MHA's website *http://mha.nic.in/fore.htm*

Which other materials on FCRA are available on the MHA's website ?

Following material on FCRA are available on MHA's website http://mha.nic.in/fore.htm ::

1. Foreign Contribution (Regulation) Act, 1976
2. Foreign Contribution (Regulation) Rules, 1976
3. Citizens charter, Charter for NGOs/Associations applying for grant of prior permission/registration under FCRA
4. Charter for NGOs/Associations granted prior permission/ registration under FCRA
5. Charter for the Chartered Accountants
6. Charter for the Banks
7. Illustrative programmes permitted to be carried out by associations having different nature
8. Check list for ensuring proper submission of applications
9. Agencies not covered by the definition of 'foreign source',
10. Common grounds for rejection of application
11. Details of registered associations
12. On-line status of pending applications
13. Annual summary on FCRA, FC forms
14. List of associations placed in prohibited category/ prior permission category u/s 6 (1), 10 (a) and 10(b) of the Act
15. Directory of officers dealing with FCRA.

Can an organisation, whose violation under FCRA has been condoned, apply for registration/prior permission ?

After the violation committed by an association has been condoned, the association can apply for prior permission (PP) only by submitting an application in form FC 1-A.

Once the PP has been granted and foreign contribution received for specific purpose has been fully/partially utilized and organisation has submitted annual FC-3 returns and accounts in prescribed format pertaining to the PP, it becomes eligible for consideration of registration under FCRA. Registration would be granted under FCRA, if other parameters are fulfilled by the association.

Can NGOs use the foreign contributions for investment in Mutual Funds and other speculative investments?

No. The foreign contributions received after prior permission/ grant of registration under the Act are to be utilized for the purpose for which they have been received and they are not to be invested in any speculative investments. Further, it is also clarified that foreign contributions can be received through a single Bank account designated for the purpose under the order for registration/ prior permission or changed thereafter with prior approval of the government.

Whether Capital Assets purchased with the help of foreign contributions can be acquired in the name of the office bearers of the association?

No. Every assets acquired out of foreign contributions should be acquired and possessed in the name of the association since association has a separate legal entity distinct from its members.

Can the NGOs/Trusts invest in profitable ventures and proceeds can be utilized for welfare activities?

No. The NGOs/Trusts should utilize the funds for the welfare purpose or related activities for which it is received. The utilization should be in line with the objectives of the association. However, foreign contributions can be utilized for self-sustaining activities, not meant for commercial purposes.

Whether interest earned out of foreign contributions be shown as fresh foreign contribution receipt during that year or not?

Yes. The interest earned out of such deposit should be shown as second / subsequent foreign contributions receipt in the FC-3 returns during the year in which it is earned.

Whether grant received from MNCs be treated as FC or not?

If the funds are received from an Indian Company incorporated under the Companies' Act, 1956 the same will not be treated as foreign contribution. But if the ownership and control rights of the company are vested in a foreign source, it will be treated as foreign contribution.

If an application for registration is submitted on-line by an NGO, does it need to submit the application in physical form also?

Yes. When an application is filed on-line, a printout of the same may be taken after submission and thereafter, it should be submitted alongwith the requisite enclosures, duly signed, to Ministry of Home Affairs.

3

Fund-raising in Developing Countries: Basic Guidelines

> Businessmen who do nothing to heighten public enthusiasm for the voluntary enterprise system are comparable to unscientific farmers who "mine" the soil, always taking something out and not using fertilizers or crop rotation to restore the good earth.
>
> —*M.S. Rukeyser*

Introduction

Some of the most frequently asked questions (FAQs) to forums for community-based organizations (CBOs) in developing countries, whatever the subject, are regarding funding.

In addition, the first impulse of many such non-governmental organization (NGO) seeking funding is to request the contact information for possible funders, and once such information is received, these NGOs often write immediately to the potential funder, stressing how desperately funds are needed. Sadly, this approach often does harm to the NGO, rather than garnering support. Not only does it rarely attract funding, it can turn funding organizations against the NGO altogether.

With all this in mind, Jayne Cravens, a consultant

based in Germany (www.coyotecommunications.com) drafted very basic tips for fund-raising for NGOs serving the developing world, as a volunteer for the Aid Workers Network (www.aidworkers.net). Several other volunteers with AWN took the draft, revised it, and posted it to AWN. However, the version you are reading now is one that has been further revised by the original author, Jayne Cravens.

The document is meant to provide very basic guidelines for small NGOs in the developing world regarding fund-raising, and to point to other, more-extensive resources; it should not, however, nor be taken as a guarantee of success for funding. Also, please note that every funding organization — corporation, foundation, government agency, etc. — has its own requirements and ways of evaluating proposals and, therefore, it is impossible to create a one-size-fits-all funding strategy. Even with these guidelines, an NGO still must do research on its own about possible funders and their grant requirements.

The Problem

The work of CBOs & NGOs in developing countries is vital to millions of peopl̃e. However, fund-raising for these organizations is particularly difficult, for numerous reasons:

- There is often great competition among numerous local groups for scarce local financial resources.
- International funders are reluctant to fund community-based NGOs "directly", because of a perception of lack of accountability, difficulty in establishing credible references, practical issues with resource transfers, and numerous tax questions.
- Some community-based organizations lack what donors regard as the necessary prerequisite

structure for being able to process donations, financial or otherwise. For many organizations, this becomes a "Catch 22": resources would permit the necessary administrative changes to become more donor rule-compliant, but they cannot get those resources without making the changes.

Fund-raising First Step - Networking & Establishing Credibility

Many funders want to know that a CBO or NGO is credible before they will even reply to an organization's request for funding. Establishing credibility doesn't take money — it takes time, effort and personal attention.

As noted earlier, the first impulse of many CBOs or NGOs seeking funding is to request the contact information for possible funders, and once such information is received, these NGOs often write immediately to the potential funder, stressing how desperately funds are needed. Sadly, this approach often harms the NGO's reputation, rather than garnering support. Not only does it rarely attract funding, it can turn funding sources against the NGO altogether.

The activity to start with for successful fund-raising is *networking*: establish relationships — formal or informal — with *local* NGOs and representatives from International NGOs, local UN offices, large employers in the area, etc. If someone were to approach any of these agencies and institutions and ask about your organization, the answers should obviously demonstrate that these other organizations know what your CBO or NGO is, why it is important, and some of the good things it has done. Having such good local relationships means its more likely for these situations to occur:

- your CBO or NGO may be able to collaborate with these organizations and institutions and, therefore, receive funding
- when funding becomes available for an activity your CBO or NGO undertakes, these organizations will contact you and let you know

To network, start locally, with:

- local reporters or local media outlets (newspaper, radio, etc.)
- large employers in your area
- local UN offices (UNDP, UNICEF, UNESCO, ITU, etc.)
- local offices for International NGOs with excellent reputations with donors, such as OneWorld, Save the Children, Oxfam, World Vision, MercyCorps, and Doctors Without Borders (this is by no means a comprehensive list)
- local CBOs and NGOs
- local communities of faith
- local universities
- international volunteers serving in your geographic area
- any associations in your area (such as associations for small businesses, associations of women farmers — such associations can be formally or informally-organized)
- local embassies or consulates
- local and regional government offices

Meet face-to-face with these people, whenever possible, to let them know what your CBO or NGO is doing — do *not* emphasize what your organization needs but, rather, the good work that it is doing, and why the organization believes its mission is important, even essential, to the area. Invite representatives of these organizations to visit your organization and see your work first hand — invite them more than once! If you can, give them printed information about your organization. And people representing your CBO or NGO should attend their events and accept their invitations too!

By doing this, you will lay the groundwork for funding! You will *greatly* increase your chances of receiving resources if you engage in these networking and reputation- building activities.

Even better is if this networking can lead to formal associations/affiliations with other local CBOs, NGOs, International NGOs, or UN agencies in your area, in the form of Memoranda of Understanding (MOUs), collaborative activities or shared resources. Potential funders view all such associations very favorably when considering who to fund.

But remember — when networking initially, do NOT ask for funds, nor describe your organization as desperate for support. The purpose of networking is to establish your organizations reputation for excellent, quality work, and to create a network of organizations and people who will verify to others that your organization is legitimate, credible and worth supporting.

Even More Credibility-Building

The aforementioned networking tips should help build up the reputation of your CBO or NGO, but there is more that you can do, if you have the resources to do such. Some of the following activities may not be possible in your geographic area, or, you may not have the funds to engage in these activities:

- *Membership in formal networks and associations* — If your country or region has a network or association of CBOs or NGOs, you should be a member. You can find these by contacting other local organizations to find out if such exists, or searching on the Internet for such.
- *Excellent online profile* — If you type your organization's name into www.google.com what happens? Does your organization's web site come up (if you have such)? What about an online document by an International NGO or UN agency that references your organization? Or a newspaper article highlighting your organization's work? Or your listing on a site such as www.onlinevolunteering.org? Anything negative come up? An online profile adds to your organization's credibility, and many potential funders, if they receive a proposal from you, will "Google" your organization's name, as well as the name of the leader of the organization, to see what comes up.

Also, post relevant information that can help others at www.developmentgateway.org, www.eldis.org and www.comminit.com. If you involve volunteers, write about how they help your CBO and NGO (especially how they help those you serve, NOT how they save you money), and submit your story to www.worldvolunteerweb.org. Even doing these activities just once every year will help *greatly* expand your online reputation, and increase the chance of your getting noticed by potential funders.

- *A clear, complete, easy-to-use web site* — It's not essential that your organization have a web site in order to attract funding, but it will help in your efforts if you do. If your organization has a web site, it should be:
- free of advertising for for-profit companies
- free of misspellings
- well-designed; simple and without lots of cumbersome graphics
- accessible via a variety of different types of web browsers
- complete, with a listing of your staff, your board of directors, your organization's address, contact information, and at least a summary of your organization's budget.
- *Academic profile* — It's not essential, but it will certainly add greatly to your organization's credibility if it has been referred to in a university-related paper. Ofcourse, it's not always possible to say yes to participation in an academic research project, given your other priorities. But your organization should try, whenever possible and when asked, to participate, as such will add to the appearance of your organization as transparent and credible to anyone investigating your organization for such.

Again, these activities may not be possible in your geographic area, or, you may not have the funds to engage in these activities. Potential funders will understand, for instance, if your CBO or NGO cannot have a web site because your resources are so limited; they will not, however, accept "limited resources" as an excuse for a web site riddled with errors, or as an excuse for negative stories about your organization online.

The Absolute Essential Preparations to Solicit Donations: Details Ready to Share

Some CBOs and NGOs are so small, so grassroots and so limited that they have no paperwork, no official documentation, and no official recognition by the government. Therefore, they must rely solely on local, in-person networking to attract local support, as most national or international funders require documentation and official recognition.

The following activities may not be possible in your geographic area, or, your CBO or NGO may not have the funds to engage in these activities, but realize that the following activities are absolutely essential to attract international funding, and sometimes more local funding as well, and being able to adapt even some of them to your situation will increase your organization's chances of receiving support. If your CBO or NGO can't do or adapt the following activities, many potential funders will feel that your organization cannot handle basic management/ governance and, therefore, is too risky to fund.

All of the following are items that most potential funders are going to want to see immediately. Therefore, do NOT start soliciting funds until you have all of the following in order and ready to share on demand:

References — Have a list of people and organizations, and their contact information (phone number, postal address, email) who are willing to affirm your organization's work and credibility, should they be contacted by potential funders. If called upon, they will verify to potential donors that your organization is worthwhile and credible. Other NGOs in your area, an international NGO serving the same geographic area, a representative from a nearby university, or a local corporation that has supported your organization in the past in some way, all make good references. The nearest UNDP office may be willing to serve as a reference for your organization as well, if they are well-acquainted with your organization's activities. Ask these organizations if they would be willing to be references regarding your organization, and to be listed in your funding proposals. Even if your NGO or CBO is so small and so resource-strapped that it cannot undertake any of the other following activities in this category of suggestions, it should, absolutely, have references.

Official papers - You need to have copies of your organization's official government documentation / registration papers (if you are, indeed, officially registered), brochures, press releases, staff list (if your staff is entirely volunteer, you still need to have a list of names of key volunteer staff) and budgets/financial statements ready for review by other organizations — or even by potential international volunteers. Potential funders will consider how quickly and completely you respond to their request for such, so get these in order and ready-to-share before you start meeting with such organizations. *Budget* - Have at least a one-page budget that shows, for last year or your most recent fiscal year:

- *expenditures* - all costs your organization incurred, even if someone donated money or paid directly to cover these costs. Expenditures should include rent, salaries, travel expenses, paper, pencils, web hosting costs — *everything*.
- *revenue* - all income, including previous donations, and that means money spent by the staff or board

or founder at the CBO or NGO for the organization (its considered, officially, a donation and, therefore, revenue).

- put the budget in your local currency *and* in either Euros or US Dollars

If you have this budget on your web site, it will add even more credibility to your organization, as it will show that you are "transparent" — a word very important to potential funders. Donors want to see accountability and transparency. They want to know how your organization's funds are spent, so they can have an idea of how a donation they make will be spent. Having this information ready to share — even sharing it unasked for with a potential donor — will demonstrate your organization's accountability and transparency.

Demonstrate That You Are Not a One-Person Organization - Donors are reluctant to fund one-person organizations. Even if the CBO or NGO has just one employee, and that employee happens to also be the founder, your organization should also involve many local volunteers, and these local volunteers should have a voice in what the CBO or NGO does, and how it works. Your written communications should demonstrate that many different people are involved in the decision-making and management of the CBO or NGO. Provide the names of people who serve on the CBO or NGO's advisory board — this may be, for instance, parents of children your organization provides services for, who help your organization make decisions about programs and strategies.

Demonstrate Quality in Communications - This means:

- written communications from your CBO or NGO stress the activities your organization undertakes successfully, and details the results the organization has achieved. The communications stress successes and the difference the organization makes in its community.

- all of the CBO or NGOs printed materials, emails and web sites are free of spelling errors, and are clear and easy to read. Otherwise, the CBO or NGO may look unprofessional to potential supporters, who are usually unwilling to fund an organization that seems as though it cannot manage basics in communication.

Don't write your communications entirely on your own with no one else helping. Recruit either local volunteers from a nearby university or business and or volunteers from transnational organizations / companies to proofread your written materials. Online volunteers are also an excellent resource to proofread and correct your materials, and can be recruited from www.onlinevolunteering.org, a free service from the United Nations Development Program.

Before Making A Funding Request

Know Your Organization

You should be very clear about what your CBO or NGO is, why it is doing the work that it does, and what it hopes to achieve. If you don't already have a statement of your CBO or NGO's overall mission and specific aims, write them down. Often, you will have only five minutes to make an initial presentation, or a potential funder will decide in the first five minutes of your presentation whether or not your CBO or NGO should be funded, so rehearse your message!

Know the Potential Donor

Research a potential donor's areas of interest, what kinds of organizations it has funded in the past, what kinds of support it's provided (financial or in kind donations of equipment, space, or staff time) and what it wants to achieve with its support.

And, *very importantly*, know the potential donor's requirements for funding proposals and apply only if you are *absolutely sure* that you can fulfill them. If you do not know the funder's details for any of the above criteria, and cannot find the information on the organization's website, ask the potential donor for clarification.

Use this information in your proposal, showing how your CBO or NGO's work fits into the potential donor's funding focus. This often impresses donors, to show that you have done research on them and know the focus of their previous funding activities.

Many donors have their own formats for proposals. If you are thinking about approaching a particular donor, always find out first if they accept uninvited applications and if they have a format. There's nothing worse than spending all that effort on a great proposal, only to find out they won't accept it, as it does not fit in their area of focus!

Have a Thank You Plan Already Defined

Prepare a plan to thank donors immediately after receiving their donations, AND, a way to update them six months after their donations about what your organization has achieved. This will increase the probability that they will contribute again!

Finding Donors & Making Contact

It can't be stressed enough — all of the above needs to be done BEFORE you begin soliciting funds!! By doing the previously-detailed activities, you greatly increase the chances of your funding proposal being accepted, and for organizations to actually approach you about funding your CBO or NGO (rather than the other way around).

Once you have undertaken the previous activities, you should be ready to begin contacting organizations specifically about funding your organization. Some basic tips about where to look and how to contact:

- Start by undertaking "donor mapping". What organizations are funding NGO activities in your geographical area? What companies are funding for-profit activities (mining, farming, ranching, etc.)? And what activities in your local community are being funded by local, regional or state government funds? These are all potential funders for a CBO or NGO. And if you engaged in the previously- detailed networking activities, they already know about your organization and its work. Once you have this informal relationship with them, you are ready to ask them about funding your organization.
- Contact embassies. They often have small grants programs, and favor organizations with whom they are already familiar (hence the importance of the previously-detailed networking activities). But be aware that these grants are often one-time-only — you cannot count on such grants to be renewed year-after-year.
- Many CBOs and NGOs in developing countries access funding from donors in other countries

through International NGO partners. And INGOs favor organizations with whom they are already familiar (hence the importance of the previously-detailed networking activities).

- Local government may be able to provide small grants. But, as many NGOs and CBOs are already aware, government funding is being scaled back in most areas, and the days of government funding all NGOs and CBOs are almost over (and are over in many places).
- UN Agencies often have small grant programs, and like others, favor organizations with whom they are already familiar (hence the importance of the previously- detailed networking activities). And often, with UN agencies, small grants can lead to more grants, and sometimes, bigger grants, in the future.
- Large transnational corporations are reluctant to fund local CBOs or NGOs serving the developing world unless the corporation has an office somewhere in or near the geographic area of the NGO. If you decide to approach a transnational corporation about funding, look at that company's web site and read *all* information posted about that company's philanthropic activities. Find out if they have an office in your geographic area. If the company has guidelines for submitting funding proposals, RESPECT THOSE GUIDELINES. If the company states that it does not fund environmental organizations, for instance, and your organization is focused on environmental issues, do not ask for funding. Also, before you solicit funding from such companies, consider creating volunteering

opportunities for that company's local employees, and invite the company's participation. These local employees, through volunteering, will get to know your organization, and may be willing to champion your organization for funding within the company.

- Foundations can be approached, but often, only through International NGO partners. Foundations usually require ALL of the items detailed under the section "The Absolute Essential Preparations To Solicit Donations: Details Ready to Share." Suggestions for how to find such foundations are noted later in this document.

When you solicit funds, stress how the funding will be used, NOT desperation for funds. Here are two examples of well-written explanations of how funds will be used:

Donations will be used to pay for the shipping of donated books from all over the world, for our library that serves disabled-children and their families. Donations will also be used to pay our two-person staff, made up of two professionals in child-development.

Donations will be used to pay the duty fees and transportation costs of five computers and networking equipment being donated to our organization by Acme Computer company, as well as to pay a local person to connect the computers to the Internet; all of this will allow us to provide Internet access to local women and children as part of our various community education activities.

Here is an example of a poorly-written explanation:

> If we do not receive donations, our doors will close!! We need fund immediately, or we must turn children away!! We urgently request your assistance!!

Remember that potential donors often have many requests for support. Don't be disheartened if they don't show interest initially.

ESSENTIAL - Respect the Organization's Granting Guidelines

It is absolutely ESSENTIAL that you find out before submitting a proposal:

- that the funder will consider projects in your country/ area/location
- that the funder will consider projects that are focused on the kind of work your CBO or NGO undertakes
- that the funder will consider funding the costs that you need (some will only fund capital expenses such as vehicles; others may only fund staff costs)
- what information the funder requires in a proposal - possibilities are detailed under the section called "The Absolute Essential Preparations To Solicit Donations: Details Ready to Share."

All funders are covered by legal documents and official policies which dictate how funds can be spent. Funders CANNOT give support outside the specifics stated on these documents. The information on what an institution will fund is often clearly stated on a funder's website.

Foundations, corporations and government offices receive hundreds of applications a month from organizations that have obviously not checked their websites. These applications not only may never receive a reply, the organizations submitting them may be marked so that any future proposals are automatically refused. The rest of this document deals with web sites that provide further information. Web addresses (URLs) change frequently. If you try a URL and it no longer works, try typing in the address to www.archive.org; or try typing in the name of the organization or resource to www.google.com to find the new URL.

Online Resources For Further Information

The website of the Synergos Institute in New York, has lots of tips on mobilizing resources. The articles are addressed to Foundations, but can be easily adapted for any of us "non-experts" engaging in periodic fund-raising. www.synergos.org/globalphilanthropy/00/fbsresources.htm

Online Resources for Detailed Tips on Writing Funding Proposals:

www.innonet.org/

The Innovation Network works with nonprofit organization to share the power of evaluation with nonprofits and funders. Their evaluation tools help with everything from creating your organization's mission statement to post-program evaluation, and draw heavily on log-framed approaches to program development.

www.ifrg.org.uk

The Resource Alliance's mission is to build the fund-raising and local resource mobilization capacity of the voluntary sector worldwide.

www.tgci.com

The Grantsmanship Center links to foundation and corporate sites of interest to fund raisers, and has general information on fund raising. Focused primarily on the USA.

www.cof.org

Council on Foundations with links to many foundations and general information on foundations and giving. Focused primarily on the USA.

http://fdncenter.org/

The Foundation Center links to foundation and corporate sites of interest to fund raisers, and provides general information on foundations and giving. Focused primarily on the USA.

www.nonprofits.org/npofaq/keywords/5o.html

Frequently Asked Questions and Answers (FAQs) regarding prospect and funder research

Online Directories of Funders

This section is not listed in the table of contents of this document. Why? Because of the original author's fear that, if it were listed, CBOs and NGOs would go straight to this section and the next section, and make the mistake frequently referred to in this document — write the potential funder "cold," having established no previous relationship and making a desperate plea for funds that can actually harm the organization's reputation with potential funders.

If you have gone through this entire document, then the following two sections are your "reward":

> United States International Grantmakers (USIG)
> www.usig.org/
> USIG seeks to facilitate international grantmaking by providing access to: recommended forms with instructions; country reports and laws, and other informational materials and resources.

The site serves both grantmakers and grantseekers to support and facilitate the process of making grants overseas.

The Grantseeker's Guide to the Internet
www.online.nonprofit.net/info.guide.html

The Foundation Directory
http://grants.library.wisc.edu/organizations/foundationsbooks.html

Funders Online (European Foundation Centre)
www.fundersonline.org/grantseekers
offers access to profiles of a vast range of international foundations' and corporate funders' websites. The Directory is also searchable by funder's areas of interest indexed by subject focus, geographic focus, population focus and types of support. The site also provides links to a variety of other pertinent funding and fund- seeking information.

There are several highly-advanced, interactive donor grant websites as well, but such charge a fee for use.

Other Funding Resources

Again, this section is not listed in the table of contents of this document, because of the original author's fear that, if it were listed, CBOs and NGOs would go straight to this section and make the mistake frequently referred to in this document — write the potential funder "cold," having established no previous relationship and making a desperate plea for funds that can actually harm the organization's reputation with potential funders.

The following list is of some very large foundations and networks that may be potential funders for your CBO or NGO, as well as online directories of foundations not already listed above.

Foundations usually require ALL of the items detailed under the section called "The Absolute Essential Preparations To Solicit Donations: Details Ready to Share." Also, as has been mentioned frequently before in this document, respect the funding guidelines of these potential funders — for instance, if an organization says it only funds environmental programs, and your organization is not an environmentally-focused organization, do NOT contact them.

AiDA (http://aida.developmentgateway.org/)
Includes historical and current information on activities of the major international development donors and some civil society organizations and private foundations.

Asian Development Bank (www.adb.org)

Charles Stewart Mott Foundation, a private philanthropy based in Flint, Michigan. www.mott.org/grants.asp

The Democracy Projects Database
http://www.ned.org/dbtw-wpd/textbase/projects-search.htm

Democracy Resource Center's 2002 Guide to Sources of Funding in International Democratic Development
http://www.ned.org/research/funding/democracyfunding.html
offers links to more than 100 foundations and other funding organizations

Fundsnet Online Services (www.fundsnetservices.com) a privately owned Web site created in 1996 for the purpose of providing Nonprofit Organizations, Colleges and Universities with information on financial resources available on the Internet.

Worldwide

Worldwide INitiatives for Grantmaker Support - WINGS (www.wingsweb.org) a network of over 40 grantmaker support organizations around the world; a meeting place for those engaged in building the infrastructure to support global philanthropy. Includes WINGS-CF, a database of organizations supporting the development and work of community foundations in different areas around the world.

Africa

Southern African Grantmakers Association - SAGA (http://wn.apc.org/)

Funding Site (The) (www.thefundingsite.co.za/)

Provides a searchable online database of prospective donors and a comprehensive range of information, training, advertising and marketing services to the South African non-profit and Development Community.

Asia

Net-NGO (www.net-ngo.com/) — an online guide to NGOs in Pakistan, and offers a links to donor organizations working in Pakistan.

Asia-Pacific Philanthropy Consortium - APPC-IC (www.asianphilanthropy.org/) serves as an information clearinghouse on the non-profit sector in the Asia-Pacific region. The website provides background information about the consortium, information about related organization, publishes an electronic Bulletin, and maintains a an on-line database of regional foundations and a database of philanthropy-related bibliography.

The Indian Centre for Philanthropy (www.indev.nic.in/icp/sicp_page_1.htm) founded in 1996, seeks to promote and strengthen philanthropy in India. The website provides detailed information about the Centre's initiatives and programs.

Japan Foundation Center (http://www.jfc.or.jp/eibun/e_index.html) The website offers an excellent overview of the Japanese foundation community and trends in philanthropy, in English; and information about the Center's work and publications, and a list of links to over 170 Japanese grantmaking organizations.

Australia

Philanthropy Australia, Inc. (www.philanthropy.org.au) the national association representing Australia's leading grantmaking private, family and corporate trusts and foundations. The website provides a wealth of information on the Association's activities, services and publications. Also included are links to the websites of Australian grantmaking organizations.

Europe

Westminster Foundation for Democracy (www.wfd.org)

The Foundation Jean Jaurès (http://fondatn7.alias.domicile.fr/affiche_site.php4) or www.jean-jaures.org (in French)

The Swedish International Liberal Centre (www.liberal-international.org)

The Alfred Mozer Foundation (www.alfredmo zerstichting.nl)

Fondation Robert Schuman (France) www.robert-schuman. org /

The Center for Philanthropy, Ukraine (http:// www.philanthropy.org.ua/) The Center aims to promote philanthropy and strengthen civil society in Ukraine.

CSR Europe (www.csreurope.org)

The European business-to-business network for Corporate Social Responsibility.

European Foundation Centre-EFC (www.efc.be)

Promotes and underpins the work of foundations and corporate funders active in and with Europe. Established in 1989 by seven of Europe's leading foundations, the has a membership of over 160 independent funders and serves a further 7,000 organizations through networking centers in 35 countries across Europe.

German Foundation Index
(http: / / www.stiftungsindex.de /)

The most comprehensive resource on German foundations on the Internet. It contains more than 150 links to German foundations' websites, a large number of reference to international grantmakers, bibliographic information on the non-profit sector and advice to grantseekers.

Maecenata Institute for Third Sector Studies
www.maecenata.de/centrum/datenbank.htm

Maintains a database on German foundations and a database on scholarships. The database on foundations offers you detailed information on 8000 German foundations. A register helps you to search for appropriate grantmaking foundations - for fund-raising and research purposes. The database on scholarships offers detailed information to students, researchers and artists on approx. 270 scholarship programs of German foundations.

Prince of Wales Business Leaders Forum (www.princeof wales.gov.uk/index.html)

An international not-for-profit organization founded, in 1990, to promote socially responsible business practices that benefit business and society and which help to achieve social, economic and environmentally sustainable development. The Forum maintains a database on socially responsible business practice.

CCINet (www.ccinet.org/)

A unique online resource about company giving, managed by Charities Aid Foundation. CCINet offers an international directory of Foundations, is dedicated to promoting learning and encouraging dialogue among funders committed to the field of organizational effectiveness.

Independent Sector (www.indepsec.org/)

A membership organization that brings together foundations, nonprofit groups and corporate giving programs to support philanthropy, volunteering and citizen action. The website provides information about the Independent Sector's programs and initiatives, membership, and publications.

Women's Funding Network (www.wfnet.org/)

A partnership between women's funds, donors and allies around the world committed to social justice. Its mission is to ensure that women's funds are recognized as the "investment of choice" for people who value the full participation of women and girls as key to strong, equitable and sustainable societies

South America

Grupo de Institutos, Fundações e Empresas (www.gife.org.br/) a membership association of institutes, foundations companies' giving web pages.

www.geofunders.org

Grantmakers for Effective Organizations (GEO), an affinity group of the Council on and corporate funders in Brazil.

North America

The National Endowment for Democracy (www.ned.org)

The International Centre for Human Rights and Democratic Development (www.ichrdd.ca/splash.html)

Canadian Centre for Philanthropy (www.ccp.ca)

A national charitable organization dedicated to advancing the role and interests of the charitable sector for the benefit of Canadian communities. The website has a special section for members only. You can further find information about the Centre's research initiatives, publications and the Centre's Imagine program.

Centro Mexicano para la Filantropía (www.cemefi.org)

The Mexican centre for philanthropy.

Council on Foundations (www.cof.org/)

An association of American foundations and corporations. The website provides detailed information about the Council's activities and services, a preview of the Council's Foundation News & Commentary magazine, and an up-to-date list of USA foundations and corporate funders with a web presence.

Foundation Center, New York (http://fdncenter.org/)

The website provides information on the FC initiatives, library services, on FC training and seminars, research and publications, as well as on grantmakers in the USA.

Funders' Network for Smart Growth and Livable Communities www.fundersnetwork.org/

A focal point for foundations, nonprofit organizations and other partners working to solve the environmental, social, and economic problems created by suburban sprawl and urban disinvestment.

Want to adapt this document? You are welcomed to translate this document into another language, edit it, change it, and republish it or distribute it, so long it is offered FOR FREE, without any charge, and you credit Jayne Cravens as the original author, her web site (www.coyotecommunications.com), and the volunteers at the Aid Workers Network as contributors, and the AFN web site (www.aidworkers.net). And it would be appreciated if you would notifmailto:jc@coyotecommunications.comthat you have done so.

II

NGOS AND OFFICIAL DONORS

In the 1950s and 1960s, Non-Governmental Organisations (NGOs) and official donors tended to pursue different development agendas. Beyond support to emergencies, they were usually disinterested in each other's activities and occasionally suspicious of the other's motives. This began to change from the early 1970s when most donors followed the earlier example of countries such as Norway and Canada in directly supporting NGO development programmes. The shift of official funding towards NGOs accelerated in the 1980s. Part of this shift is explained by the growth in emergency assistance in the period but it also reflected a growing recognition of the role of NGO programmes in meeting official aid objectives in areas such as poverty reduction, environmental conservation, health and education.

The Financial Contribution

One of the most tangible indicators of growing interaction has been the change in the quantity of funds official aid agencies channel to and through NGOs for their *development* activities. Figures from the Organisation for Economic Cooperation and Development (OECD) indicate that the total amount of official aid going to NGOs for development in 1992/93 was US$2.2bn, while data from the World Bank put the 1992 figure at $2.5bn. Why do these figures seriously underestimate actual flows?

The financial contribution of donors to NGO development activities is commonly presented in terms of two ratios:

- the proportion of official aid channelled to NGOs

- the contribution of official aid funds to total NGO income.

Published OECD data suggest that in aggregate about 5% of all official aid is now channelled to NGOs. Not only are these figures an underestimate, but they fail to capture wide variation among different donors in the share of official aid going to and through NGOs. For individual donors, the ratio ranges from less than 1% for some donors to up to 30%

Published aggregate figures indicate more accurately the growing importance of donor funds to overall NGO income: the World Bank judges that whereas in the early 1970s about 1.5% of total NGO income came from donor sources, by the mid-1990s this share had risen to about 30%. Yet these figures, too, conceal wide variations across donor countries, ranging from about 10% of total NGO income to 80% or more.

Also of importance has been the pace at which donors have increased the funds they channel to NGOs. For instance, in the ten years to 1993/94, the United Kingdom increased its official funding of NGOs by almost 400% to £68.7m, raising the share of total aid channelled to NGOs from 1.4% to 3.6%. In the same period, Australia increased its official funding of NGOs from A$20m to A$71m, raising the share of total aid going to NGOs from 1% to 6%. Similar expansion occurred in the case of Finland, Norway and Sweden from the early 1980s to the early 1990s.

Funding Arrangements

In terms of donor-NGO funding arrangements, there are variations across countries. In Australia, there are 32 different funding mechanisms through which NGOs can obtain funds from the Government. However, the dominant type of NGO activity funded by donors today remains projects and programmes put forward for funding by the NGOs themselves, and utilised for projects and programmes in particular developing countries. In the United Kingdom, this is through the Overseas Development Administration's (ODA) Joint Funding Scheme; in Sweden, through the NGO Programme; in Finland, through the NGO Support Programme. Additionally, a small proportion of donor funds are channelled through a range of international NGOs, while most bilateral donors have also provided funds to NGOs specialising in sending volunteers abroad, and to NGOs working on education and information initiatives within donor countries.

All donors have introduced criteria to determine the eligibility of potential projects put up for funding: some use sectoral specialists to review project proposals, others provide funds almost on a self-monitoring basis within general guidelines. Donors vary, too, in the share of total project costs which donors are willing to fund, from 50% or less (the UK) to 75% and upwards (Finland, Sweden). Donors have also differed in the relationship between the level of funds requested by the NGOs and the official funds available: some parliaments (Sweden) have, until very recently, repeatedly voted more funds each year than there are projects available to fund. Others (such as the UK) have to reject a high proportion of projects, because of a shortage of total funds allocated.

Different donors have also applied varying degrees of conditionality on the non-project funds they provide for NGO work. In contrast to the United Kingdom, which has stringent conditions attached to official funds used for development education and information work, other donors, such as the Scandinavians, have a more permissive approach and even provide funds for activities and campaigns critical of official aid policy.

The Role of NGOs in Donor Programmes

What all these particular funding schemes have in common is that they are official contributions to the NGOs' own development projects and programmes. Increasingly in recent years, however, NGOs have been co-opted to assist official aid agencies execute donors' own projects and programmes. For these types of initiative it is usual for donors to contribute all the funds required to execute these particular projects effectively on a 'sub-contract' basis. Although aggregate data on the amount of official funds channelled to these types of initiative have not been gathered, country studies conducted by the ODI indicate that, in recipient countries with a large and growing NGO presence, 5% and more of total bilateral aid funds are commonly used for these NGO sub-contracted initiatives.

There are three factors which have influenced donors to utilise the skills and services of NGOs to help further their own agenda.

- First, donors have been using NGOs to support their emergency and relief activities for some time, so providing funds for NGO development projects has often been viewed as a natural progression.
- Second, poor performance of official donor programmes in reaching the poor and carrying out successful rural development projects in the late 1960s and 1970s, married with the clear popularity of NGOs for their work in the fields of education and health, and claims by NGOs that they were able to reach the poor and improve their lives, has

led donors to turn to NGOs to help them achieve a greater poverty focus in their own aid programmes.

- Third, and relatedly, donors have seen NGOs as a means of getting around obstacles to aid impact caused by inefficient and corrupt governments, as well as a way of reaching people in those countries where they had suspended official aid programmes.

Official Donors and Southern NGOs

Historically, most official funds have gone to support the work of NGOs based in donor countries, even though the bulk of the funds have been spent in developing countries. An early reason for this was that there were few viable, and effective, indigenous NGOs. Yet over the past 15 years there has been rapid growth in the number, as well as the capabilities of NGOs based in developing countries: *southern* NGOs.

The growth of southern NGOs has varied from country to country but, in general, effective southern NGOs emerged earliest in south and east Asia (such as Bangladesh and the Philippines) and in a number of countries in Latin America such as Chile, Brazil and Nicaragua. Only in the last ten years has there been a rapid growth in the number and importance of indigenous NGOs in Africa and their influence varies markedly across countries.

The donor view which saw increasing merit in working through NGOs, together with the growing strength of southern NGOs, has led more and more donors to supplement their support of northern NGOs with direct funding of southern NGOs. Such donor-NGO initiatives became prominent in the early 1980s and have continued to expand thereafter.

In 1988, the ODA channelled £3.4m to 40 Bangladesh health-related NGOs under the Bangladesh Population and Health Consortium, and over a five year period to 1993 has provided over £5m to a large NGO in Bangladesh, the Bangladesh Rural Advancement Committee. The United States, Canada, Norway and Sweden are amongst the leading bilateral donors who have all channelled substantial funds to local NGOs, with a heavy concentration in south Asia. The EC and the UNDP have been among the leading multilateral agencies to fund southern NGO activities.

Mirroring the support given to northern NGOs, official funding of southern NGOs has taken two forms: the funding of initiatives put forward by southern NGOs, and the utilisation of the services of southern NGOs to help donors achieve their own aid objectives.

Early moves by donors to fund southern NGOs directly have often been viewed with misgivings by northern NGOs. Yet when donors have embarked on this type of initiative in consultation with their home-based NGOs, and especially when they have used the experience of northern NGO personnel on the ground to assist these direct funding initiatives, the process has often stimulated northern NGOs to assess their own comparative advantage and has been welcomed.

Donor funding of southern NGOs has received a mixed reception from recipient governments. Clear hostility from many non-democratic regimes has been part of more general opposition to any initiatives to support organisations beyond the control of the state. But even in democratic countries, governments have often resisted moves seen as diverting significant amounts of official aid to non-state controlled initiatives, especially where NGO projects have not been integrated with particular line ministry programmes.

The Rise of the 'Reverse Agenda'

The growth in official donor support to NGOs has not always been welcome to NGOs. Reluctance by many northern NGOs to accept large amounts of official aid funds has been based on two mutually-reinforcing ideas: that their development approach was qualitatively different from that of the official aid agencies, and that, as donors continued to apply conditions to funds channelled to NGOs, a rise in donor funding would increasingly be likely to compromise the integrity of NGO approaches to development.

Using NGOs to help achieve donors' own aid objectives only heightened these concerns, though the degree of concern has always varied across different donor countries. For example, in most Scandinavian countries, NGOs have received from the state upwards of 80% of income for their projects and most have not felt their integrity threatened as a result. Some major US NGOs, on the other hand, have refused to consider official funding.

Though NGO anxiety about being over-run by the official donor agenda has persisted, the growing role and status of NGOs has fuelled a different phenomenon, increasingly referred to as the *reverse agenda*. This is the process whereby the approach and methods of the NGOs are now influencing the activities and perceptions of donors and official aid programmes, in some cases as a direct result of donors seeking out NGO ideas.

There are a number of ways in which this has manifested itself. For instance, some of the characteristics of the 'NGO approach' to development participatory planning, assessing a gender dimension, and concern with the environment have gradually been incorporated into mainstream donor thinking. Additionally, some donors (such as Australia,

Germany, the Netherlands and Norway) regularly seek out the views of NGOs in drawing up particular official bilateral aid programmes: Norway did this in 1993 for their programmes in Ethiopia and Nicaragua. Of particular interest has been the willingness of the World Bank (which has often attracted the hostility of NGOs) to engage in discussions with NGOs and to include some NGOs in the implementation of World Bank projects

A direct effect of the growing influence of the reverse agenda has been to increase the common ground between donors and NGOs. No longer is it easy to talk of distinct differences between NGO and donor approaches to development.

One manifestation of a growing common ground has been the way that most donors have broadened their aid objectives. Thus, most donors now include poverty alleviation, concern with the environment and enhancing the status of women as major aid objectives. Perhaps of even greater importance is that most donors now view action to enhance human rights and democratic processes as a constituent part of their development agenda. Additionally, many donors have taken up 'strengthening civil society' as a specific aid objective. This is doubly beneficial to NGOs both because NGOs are seen to constitute an important part of civil society, and because one of the core objectives of NGOs has been to work to 'empower' poor people, especially by strengthening the organisations to which poor people belong.

One concrete result of a growing overlap of objectives is that donors themselves are now increasingly willing to bring those projects and programmes, which for a long time were typically initiated by NGOs, within the umbrella of official aid. It is now not uncommon for donors to take over (and often expand) the funding of projects in the developing countries which were started and have been funded by (usually northern) NGOs.

Though these examples provide evidence of a widening cluster of initiatives where it is no longer possible to make a strong and clear distinction between donors and NGOs in terms of project approach and execution, it is important not to press the common agenda argument too far. Thus a number of NGOs, including a high proportion of the long established and larger northern NGOs and a growing number of southern NGOs, remain wary of these recent developments and are still concerned to maintain their distance from donors. Some argue that the growing convergence of the NGO and official aid agenda could well turn out to be more a convergence of *language* about development than convergence in the overall approach to development. In particular many large international NGOs remain extremely critical of donors' support for economic policy reform (or structural adjustment) programmes.

The Future

The common ground between donors and NGOs can be expected to grow, especially as donors seek to make more explicit their stated objectives of enhancing democratic processes and strengthening marginal groups in civil society. However, and in spite of a likely expansion and deepening of the reverse agenda, NGOs are likely to maintain their wariness of too close and extensive an alignment with donors.

In aggregate, the direct funding of southern NGOs by donors, now emerging as a significant form of interaction, is likely to expand in the next few years, even though some donors (such as Norway) may not follow this trend.

Ironically, this expansion could well be accompanied by greater involvement of northern NGOs and northern NGO personnel, by contracting them to help administer and monitor the impact of such funds. This is in part because many officials of donor agencies often do not have the skills and expertise necessary to liaise effectively with the often small and dispersed organisations which make up the southern NGO 'community'. It might be assumed that these trends will result in increased funding of NGOs by donors in the years ahead.

For growing numbers of northern NGOs, such an expansion would help to compensate for what appears to be falling aggregate income from private (non-official) sources (down to $5.4bn in 1994, compared with $6bn in 1992). However a new, if very recent, phenomenon is that some donors who have provided large amounts of money to NGOs (Canada, Sweden and Finland) have announced cuts of 10% or more. In contrast, USAID intends to channel 40% of its bilateral resources through NGOs by the end of the century, up from 34% in 1994. In general, however, where donors have started to cut aid to NGOs, this has mainly been due to overall pressure on, and often absolute cuts in, the aggregate aid budget, in some cases reflecting doubts about the entire aid enterprise in the post-Cold War era.

Together these differing trends may enable donors and NGOs to cooperate even more closely than in the past. If a deeper sense of mutual interests and mutual purpose between donor agencies and NGOs does emerge, this might lead NGOs to devote less energy and fewer resources to criticising those aspects of the donor agenda they dislike, and more to building and widening the common ground they increasingly share.

III

FUNDING ARRANGEMENTS WITH NON-GOVERNMENT ORGANISATIONS

We live in an era of collaboration and partnership between the Government and communities, where the Government makes policy choices on the spending of public money and the services are increasingly delivered by NGOs in the private and voluntary sectors. There is broad consensus about the involvement of NGOs in publicly funded service delivery, and the importance of values such as collaboration and mutual trust between the Government and NGOs. This has been reflected in a number of developments, including an agreed statement of government intentions towards the voluntary sector.

Nevertheless, there are expectations of transparency and accountability, and the best use of public money. A collaborative approach does not, on its own, ensure either transparency or accountability. There are tensions between collaboration and mutual trust on the one hand, and control and strict enforcement of contractual performance on the other hand.

With justifiably high expectations of accountability over the use of public funds, more relaxed controls create substantial risks for both the Government and NGOs.

Since 2000, when a range of issues were raised relating to the Waipareira Trust[1], we have been extensively involved in issues relating to contract and other funding arrangements between the Government and NGOs.

In our 2003 report of an inquiry into the management of funding arrangements with several NGOs connected with Donna Awatere Huata MP[2] ("the Huata inquiry"), we outlined some of our expectations of how public entities contracting with NGOs, or providing funding to them, should ensure proper accountability, transparency, and best use of public money. Parts of the inquiry report have been used as a *de facto* best-practice guide, although it was not written to be so.

Based on our experience from this and other studies, we have identified several risk areas, including particularly:

- scrutiny of the governance and management capability of the potential provider;
- monitoring of the arrangements with the provider; and
- review of whether the arrangements have the desired impact.

We have advocated a risk-management approach. Policies and standard procedures should be designed to mitigate risks that are systemic and common to this type of funding arrangement. This should be done in ways that are most cost effective for the funding entity, and most efficient in terms of transaction and compliance cost for the NGO. Key and critical risks in the funding arrangements should be identified and mitigated, with resources being re-allocated where necessary to ensure that the higher level of risk is mitigated.

Since the Huata inquiry, we have continued to be involved in NGO issues across a range of government agencies, particularly in the health, social services and education sectors, including providing best-practice advice. We have also contributed to several forums on this issue.

Treasury Guidelines

The Treasury has issued *Guidelines for Contracting with Non-Government Organisations for Services Sought by the Crown* (the Guidelines). The Guidelines are intended to encourage better contracting practices by all departments and Crown entities involved in negotiating arrangements with NGOs for services that support the Government's objectives. The Guidelines were first issued in 2001, and were updated in 2003.

The Guidelines cover the following aspects of the contract lifecycle:

- planning;
- selecting a provider;
- negotiating the contract;
- managing the contract;
- review and evaluation; and
- starting over.

The Guidelines do not diminish the need for government agencies to exercise informed judgement about the arrangements that may be appropriate in their own circumstances. The Treasury is clear that the Guidelines are not a manual on how to write contracts.

What we plan to do

During our recent cycle of strategic audit planning, we further developed and refined our work programme in relation to the issues surrounding NGOs. We have identified the NGO area as one that would benefit from an integrated audit approach. We set out our intentions below.

2004-05

During 2004-05, we intend to continue to provide wider assurance to public entities on their NGO-funding activities where appropriate.

We will continue to highlight NGO issues with our appointed auditors through the audit briefs we issue. Our auditors have been asked to ensure that public entities within the Crown reporting entity that contract with NGOs are fully aware of our best-practice recommendations arising from the Huata inquiry, and the Treasury guidelines.

We have asked our auditors to review the quality of departments' and Crown entities' contract management systems in the course of the 2004-05 annual audit, to ensure that they are consistent with the Treasury guidelines – with a particular focus on the adequacy of the monitoring and audit arrangements in place to ensure that services purchased are properly delivered. Any audit concerns will be reported to the public entity in the management letter, and, where appropriate, to the Minister and the relevant Select Committee as part of the financial review.

2005-06

In 2005-06, we intend to develop a best-practice guide on our audit expectations of NGO contracting and funding arrangements. We will use the knowledge and expertise built up over recent years to develop our audit expectations. In developing those expectations, we expect to have discussions with central agencies, and we will take account of the Treasury guidelines.

We also intend to establish the specific work we could usefully carry out on NGO issues as part of annual audits.

We expect that this work will link closely to our best-practice expectations.

2006-07 onwards

In 2006-07 and future years, we intend to reflect the outcomes of our research and development work in annual audits. We also intend to institute a rolling performance audit programme examining different agencies' management of NGO contracting arrangements, using our best-practice expectations as audit criteria.

4

NGOs and Conflict Resolution

> Most controversies would soon be ended, if those engaged in them would first accurately define their terms, and then adhere to their definitions.
>
> — *Tryon Edwards*

With the multiplication and escalation of conflicts at various levels, the need for conflict resolution has become urgent than ever before. There has been a government realization among governments, international organization and non-governmental organization that more resources and time need to be set apart for managing conflicts and that the work for peace has to place by harnessing the cooperation of several agencies at different levels. Governments by virtue of their rigid structure very often failed to address adequately questions related to conflicts of a delicate and complex nature. Also failed agencies and resources available with governments have been founding inadequate in this respect. The latest tendency is to search for other tracks of conflict resolution and also resources to compliment government effort.

Multi-Track Approach

The movement from 'track — one diplomacy' (1) to 'track - two diplomacy' (2) resulted in the emergency of a large number of actors in conflict resolution and peace building process. John McDonald and Louis Diamond have identified nine actor categories or tracks in conflict resolution: official diplomacy, education, research and training, business, funding, media and communication, religion, NGOs and advocacy groups and private citizens (3) In addition to these group of actors the Carnegie Commission recognized the role of the UN and religion organizations in peace building process (4) Barnett Rubin and Susana Campbell in a study for the Canter for Preventive Action pointed out that "the multiplicity and variety of actors involved in generating conflicts requires a similar multiplicity of international partners to resolve them" (5) Multidimensional nature of conflicts has been partly in giving rise to the concept of a multi-track approach in conflict resolution.

Diamond and McDonald say that multi-track diplomacy is "a conceptual framework designed .... to reflect the variety of activities that contribute to international peacemaking". They pointed out that track two diplomacy is designed (1) to reduce or resolve conflict between groups or nations by improving communications, understanding and relationships; (2) to lower tension, anger, fear or misunderstanding by humanizing and "face of the enemy" and giving people direct personal experience of one another; (3) to affect the thinking and action of track-one (i.e. official diplomacy) by exploring diplomacy options without prejudice, thereby preparing the ground for move formal negotiations for re-framing policies. The successful resolution of conflict mainly depends on track — two diplomacy complimenting track - one diplomacy. Thus a combined effort of track-one and track-two becomes in t he process of conflict resolution.

NGOs and International Agencies

Over the years there has been a tremendous increase

in the number of NGOs., so also the variety of their activities and their geographical spread. Because most of the NGOs are involved in works relating to development, relief and advocacy, which are of direct and visible benefit to the people, they have achieved a high degree of good will. In addition, many of the NGOs have skilled personnel who can intervene in conflict situations creatively in order to bring resolution. This fact has been recognizes by the United Nations as well as international funding agencies like the World Bank who now bank upon the resources of NGOs for conflict resolution, particularly in areas like early warning, third party intervention, reconciliation, particularly in areas like early warning, third party intervention, reconciliation and peace building.

The UN General Assembly recognized the role of NGOs and called upon the UN Department of Public Information (DPI) to work with NGOs interested in communicating information about the United Nations. In continuation of the General Assembly resolution, the NGOs and Institutional Relations Section was established within DPI to provide information and other liaison services to the growing number of NGOs accredited to the United Nations. In 1968, the UN Economic and Social Council formalized its consultative relationship with NGOs. However it is to be noted that NGOs were not given any formal status in the General Assembly or other powerful bodies like the Security Council.

As witnessed now NGOs have become key partners in development assistance especially to less developed countries from international agencies like the UN, the European Union and the World bank. Boutros Boutros-Ghali, former Secretary General of the UN affirmed that NGOs “are an indispensable part of the legitimacy without which no international activity can be meaningful.

The Role of NGOs

NGOs constitute an essential part of civil society and they have the potential to play key roles in resolving conflicts and restoring civil society. NGOs can support to form well knit local infrastructures or peace constituencies comprising of people from different sectors of civil society whose aim is to attain sustainable peace and whose activities are based on long term commitment. NGOs should invest more resources for capacity building activities at different levels. It involves the training of own staff, identifying indigenous partners, local leaders and so on, NGOs can act as mediators to bring consensus among different conflicting groups with the help of local peace constituencies.

Pamela Aall suggests a number of roles that NGO's can play in the peace making process. NGOs should presume their traditional relief and rehabilitation activities with a long-term perspective. "The initial emergency relief response should be linked to a set of activities that leads to the transformation of those conflicts in a way that promotes sustained and comprehensive reconciliation among the warring parties". Aall cautions us against the dangers of using external resources in relief and rehabilitation activities. Excessive use of external resources can foster dependence and passivity. It can also become a new object of contention, inadvertently fueling the conflict. NGOs should mobilize local resources which empower the people and enroll new participants into their activities, especially women who have often been kept passive in the peace process. NGOs should continue to monitor human rights abuses. They should undertake the task of providing an early warning of potentially violent conflicts and should pursue conflict resolution activities.Aall warns that these roles must be kept separate both of the safety of NGO workers and in order for it to be effective.

Prerequisites

To work effectively in a conflicting situation NGOs should preserve their own identities and neutrality and should appear to be impartial. Unofficial status of NGOs provides more access to conflicting parties, which helps in the process of negotiation. The long-term commitment of NGOs is a crucial factor in establishing trust among the people and to attend to the goal of lasting peace. Pamela A all prescribes four conditions for NGOs more directly engaging in conflict resolution activities: (1) the NGO must be very familiar with the country, issues and participants in the conflict (2) the NGO should have indigenous partners (3) NGO staff must be well grounded in conflict resolution skills and knowledge and (4) NGO workers must understand and accept the personal risk they run in attempting to intervene directly in the conflict.

Summing Up

State is often seen as one of the parties in a large number of conflicts. Therefore, it is important for NGOs to maintain their independence without loosing trust of the conflicting parties including the state. NGOs should work in co-operation and co-ordination with each other to reduce duplication in their activities. In this process NGOs should not loose their individual identities. Coordination and networking of NGOs is a key factor in lobbying and advocacy at a higher level... NGOs should limit their scope of work to mere conflict resolution, but expand to address the root causes of conflict and enhance the process of peace building. Hence, the role of the NGOs in conflict resolution is based on their presence at the ground level as actors with a reservoir of good will generated through years of development and rehabilitation work. Apart from creating a congenial atmosphere for negotiations, where the prospects for such negotiations are not visible at the level of the conflicting actors, the NGOs can play a key role in many intractable conflicts. Peace building is now seen as a part of sustaining agreements reached. No organization is perhaps more equipped that the NGOs in undertaking this task. However, in order to play a more effective role in conflict management, the NGOs may have to reorient themselves with the requisite and attitude and skills, which of course should be seen as an additional element of their development work.

(Courtesy: S.K. Joseph)

5

NGOs and Financing Dilemma

> **Never** make a decision yourself, if you don't have to. When one of your men asks you a question, ask him what is the answer. There is only one answer to many questions, and therefore, this method answers many questions before they are asked. It not only develops your men, but also enables you to measure their ability.
>
> —*Henry L. Doherty*

I

Northern development NGOs are increasingly dependent on official funds to realise their civic agenda. This partly reflects their popularity as alternative channels of aid delivery, partly the stagnation of private gifts accruing to them. Only a few NGOs reject public funding on principle. The changing nature of government support compounds the problem. Throughout the OECD, donor agencies are earmarking funds to special programmes (e.g. on democratisation, women, the environment). Northern NGOs can apply for these funds, but there are generally conditions attached to them. This also means that there is less money available for NGOs to finance their own initiatives.

This dependency presents a rather paradoxical situation for civil society organisations that are fiercely attached to their own values and autonomy of action. It causes tensions between NGOs and governments, reflected in vivid debates on autonomy, subcontracting and complementarity. At best, NGOs fear a loss of freedom and flexibility. At worst, they see themselves being co-opted by governments as cheap executing agencies.

NGO-financing

Governments in different Northern countries have developed various ways to support NGOs. At the lowest level, they provide indirect support by allowing tax deductions for private donations. Most countries, however, have developed co-financing schemes to match funds raised by NGOs themselves. Sometimes, funds are earmarked for specific components of NGO work such as transport, personnel, or even for the Government/NGO-dialogue.

Four distinct approaches to government sponsorship for NGO-activities can be identified: the programme approach, the project approach, the 'window' approach, and the 'quango' approach (each of which is analysed below). In most countries, they are taken care of by a single ministry for Development Cooperation. NGOs often use the four approaches in a mix to finance their varied operations. This might be a surprise since each of these approaches to NGO sponsorship differs in its origins, underlying philosophy and consequences for the autonomy, working methods and even the development actions of an NGO.

The four approaches can be placed on a continuum. At the liberal end, there is the Programme Approach. At the other and most restrictive end, is the so-called 'quango' approach (i.e. quasi-autonomous NGO Approach).

As the table shows, the roles of government and NGOs in initiating action, in executing projects and in financing varies between the different approaches.

Quango Approach

All previous approaches leave the initiative to the NGOs. It is their choice if they want to ask for government money and if they want to accept the strings attached. Under the quango approach, governments consciously utilise NGOs to execute projects aimed at achieving government objectives. These quasi-autonomous NGOs thus become mere executing agencies. They are called upon for their flexibility, their better contacts with certain target groups, their cheap delivery of services or their experience and professionalism. The objectives and the strategies of the development actions implemented by the subcontracting quangos are determined by the governmental funding agency.

Project Approach

Few governments have developed a programme approach which is based on mutual trust. Most have institutionalised their scepticism and discomfort with NGOs by adopting project approaches. Proposals are scrutinized on a case-by-case basis, by public servants who check if the proposed activity falls within governmental priorities and if it is 'politically acceptable'. The negative side-effects of this approach have become apparent. NGOs and their partners in Africa, Asia or Latin America have to rely on ever more creative packaging to suit the system. The NGO's own identity and social project may find itself diluted in favour of a hotchpotch of isolated activities, that donors are willing to fund. It may also lead to a growing bureaucratisation of the NGO sector.

Programme Approach

A government relying on a programme approach, accepts the existence and free development of a civil movement which is concerned about North-South problems. Because government positively appreciates the value, representativeness and effectiveness of NGOs, it provides them with funds - on a contractual basis - to execute their activities. NGO efforts are seen as a complementary contribution to the government's own policies and programmes (e.g. in development education). A strong NGO sector, in turn, is perceived as broadening political support for development cooperation. This approach is very much inspired by the public sponsoring systems for traditional civic movements (involved in labour, youth and adult education, health care, etc).

Window Approach

A window approach is less appreciative of the specificity of the NGOs than the programme and project approaches. Here, governments elaborate their own diversified strategies for tackling development problems and invite outside actors, including NGOs, to present concrete project proposals for financing. Well-known examples are the specific budgetlines for gender projects, human rights, democratisation and the environment. In this system, NGOs compete with private consultants, research institutes and national organisations all trying to get the same scarce resources.

Responses of NGO

As is being witnessed everywhere, NGO financing patterns are changing in most OECD countries. Some governments are both flexible and prepared to provide multi-year programme financing. Others adopt a more conditional and restrictive approach and prefer window and quango types of support.

Northern NGOs are responding in different ways to these challenges on their autonomy and funding base:

'Follow the Market'

A second category of NGOs links its survival and growth to the market. The priorities of these NGOs are increasingly determined by prevailing market opportunities and special funds rather than by constituencies. In some cases, this has led NGOs to become private firms, tendering for government contracts. Other NGOs see the market as a means to earn untied money (e.g. by setting up trading associations like Oxfam). In principle, there is nothing wrong with a more market-oriented approach. It may lead to quick and cost-effective responses to genuine needs (e.g. emergency aid). But this approach may also induce NGOs to become too 'greedy' and obsessed with financial growth rather than with development impact, innovation and political work. It may increase (unfair) competition among NGOs. Governments prefer to do business with NGOs acting as subcontracting agencies than with those displaying a political agenda and critical watchdog attitudes.

'Close your eyes'

This seems to be the implicit strategy pursued by several Northern NGOs. These are usually dogmatically attached to their autonomy and reluctant to accept change. They blame the government for being intrusive while refusing to co-operate with other NGOs (seen as competitors), or with official aid agencies (seen as the enemy). This strategy offers few perspectives for efficient action in the field and institutional survival at home. It leads to a proliferation of small, generalist NGO's, scrambling for projects and gifts.

'Specialise'

Some Northern NGOs believe that specialisation is the best guarantee to ensure both greater development impact and institutional survival. In an increasingly complex world, knowledge and expertise are highly valued. The development agenda has expanded dramatically, thus creating new opportunities for NGOs that have specialised skills to offer in certain niches. The rapid growth of NGOs in the South also compels Northern NGOs to show that they have a real added-value to offer (beyond the provision of funds). Experience so far suggests that specialist NGOs will have little problem in securing their funding needs on a relatively autonomous basis.

'Move Towards Internationalisation'

Internationalisation is high on the agenda of several Northern NGOs. This strategy is a two-edged sword. It has great potential if it is done to overcome chronic problems of scale, duplication and competition for dwindling funds. Through larger entities, Northern NGOs may develop the critical mass of funds and skills required to influence policy. But internationalisation can also be used by Northern NGOs to ensure their own (financial) survival. The risk of reduced funding at home is circumvented by diversifying funding sources from abroad. According to Ian Smillie, this may lead to a situation in which international NGOs 'do to older and smaller NGOs what McDonald's does to established restaurants when it moves into a neighbourhood: they put them out of business'.

'Put Identity Before Autonomy'

A large group of NGOs reject both a sterile attachment to the principle of autonomy and a too market-oriented approach. In their view, NGOs are more than cheap delivery systems. They see themselves as independent actors, with a specific role to play in international cooperation and in their own societies.

To achieve their objectives, however, they will have to make some hard choices. The first is to remain unambiguously in the civic realm. Funding that reshapes NGOs into parastatals or private firms should be avoided. The second is to put identity before autonomy. This means investing heavily in refining their own mandate, role, funding strategies, in-house skills and expertise. Thirdly, having clarified their identity, they need to build strategic alliances with a wide variety of other actors (such as governments, trade unions, social movements, private sector associations and local authorities). For too long, development NGOs have worked in 'splendid isolation' in both the North and the South. This is a luxury that can no longer be afforded. According to Thomas Dichter: 'All the necessary ingredients for an effective aggregation of the players in development are present, perhaps for the first time... Perhaps what is needed now is a balancing, an articulation of the parts'. Northern NGOs with a clear identity may have the best chances of find their niche within this new configuration.

Future Challenges

It is rather hazardous to speculate about the future of the Northern NGO sector. Most of the premises, underlying their activities, are in a process of rapid change. Development problems are becoming increasingly complex. Roles and responsibilities of Northern NGOs are being questioned by their Southern partners. There are doubts about impact and sustainability. Sources of secure finance are under pressure. And unconditional support from public opinion is no longer guaranteed.

Against this background, the most promising strategy for NGOs seems to rest on developing a strong identity. Northern NGOs that are firmly rooted in their own societies (e.g. in social movements) and that provide clear added value, will probably have less to fear from government co-option, market regulation or direct funding.

For this scenario to prevail, some other thorny issues will have to be resolved. First, how to reduce the unhealthy competition among Northern NGOs for public opinion support? This leads to a proliferation of fund-raising appeals, often based on miserable images of Third World countries. Here also, developmental NGOs with a sound message are in no position to compete with those promoting relief or child sponsoring. Second, how to provide incentives for NGOs to abandon their almost exclusive focus on local NGOs and to work together with a wide variety of development actors? This holds major promise for greater development impact and sustainability. Third, how to build new partnerships between Northern NGOs and their governments, based on mutual respect for each partner's identity and role?

In each of the three cases, the way in which government funds are used is a most critical factor. If carefully managed, they can provide powerful incentives for increased co-operation among NGOs, diversification of partnerships in the field and a new relationship with governments.

II

MANAGING GLOBALIZATION

Tsunami. Hurricane. Earthquake. War. If you're a charitable aid organization, the past couple of years have been busy. But globalization has presented charitable groups with new opportunities, albeit with one or two challenging side effects.

The new developments start from square one: getting

the message out. The advent of international 24-hour news channels and Internet sites for all kinds of media outlets has made it easier for aid groups to alert potential donors, said Jo Leadbeater, head of policy for Oxfam, the international aid and lobbying group based in Britain.

"Our work is much more in people's living rooms," she said, when a crisis happens. "You've got pictures and journalists who also are there within the first two hours. We get people ringing us to say, 'We saw the media coverage you had around the Pakistan earthquake,' or Lebanon, and they want to give money."

The thirst for news has kept crises and emergencies in the spotlight. "From the tsunami on, we've had a pretty regular stream of international emergencies that have kept people pretty clued in," said Jeremy Barnicle, communications director for Mercy Corps, the relief group based in Portland, Oregon. "People thought that there was going to be donor fatigue. On the contrary, our funding has gone through the roof since then. People have stayed with us and stayed engaged."

Fund-raising has also changed. Where once aid groups used to raise money in wealthy countries and then use it to help people in poor countries, now the distinction is not as clear. "For a group like us," Barnicle said, "that works globally, there's no reason why we shouldn't raise money globally."

Many groups have aid projects in India, but now Mercy Corps is looking at the country, and at China, as places to raise money. And Leadbeater said Oxfam was "doing a lot of thinking about how do we fund-raise in new markets like India, where there's a burgeoning middle class, or South Africa or Brazil."

Global communications networks have made lobbying easier, too, Leadbeater said. Teleconferencing with teams in Africa, Asia, Europe and North America has helped Oxfam to target politicians and officials with barrages of information and appeals. On-the-ground operations are also benefiting from globalizing technologies such as voice-over-internet telephony. "To have a technology like that," Barnicle said, "where people can talk to each other for free or really cheap, actually lets us be much more efficient with donor dollars."

Being better connected, through information networks as well as transport links, has also helped to get aid where it is needed. "Largely, in emergencies, we can respond faster," Leadbeater said. "We can basically start a humanitarian response on day one. That's made so much easier by the fact that information flows that much faster, and that we've got regional teams that can respond that much quickly - and also that so many places are just more accessible."

Globalization has also had a tremendous impact on Oxfam's human resources, thanks to a much broader recruiting base. "Among our expat staff, it's way more diverse than it would have been 20 years ago," Barnicle said. In Darfur, Sudan, Barnicle said, he encountered a Mercy Corps team that included a Tajik, a Bulgarian, two Kenyans and an Iranian. "If you'd visited a program like that 10 or 15 years ago," Barnicle said, "it would have been a Canadian, an American, an Australian."

III

NONPROFIT RESOURCES

Nonprofit Corporation Compliance Issues

- Nonprofit Corporations generally file for Tax Exemption from the IRS. This exemption carries some requirements, namely:
  - o Annual filing of Form 990
  - o Abstaining for all political campaigning
  - o Enganing in only limited lobbying
  - o No private benefit, particularly to members and officers of the corporation
  - o Transfer of the assets to a charitable purpose when the corporation dissolves
  - o Activities unrelated to the organization's purpose are taxable (UBIT)
- Many states have requirements for nonprofit organizations, including:
  - o Registering with the Attorney General
  - o Registering and reporting on fundraising activities
  - o Filing an annual report
  - o Rcporting any significant transfer of assets out of the state of incorporation

Nonprofit Corporation Checklist

- Research goals and mission
- Develop a plan and recruit board members
- Establish Corporation

  - o Adopt Articles of Incorporation and File with the State
  - o Name the Board of Directors and adopt Bylaws
  - o Obtain an EIN - Tax ID number by filing form SS-4 with the IRS
  - o Obtain Tax Exempt status by filing Form 1023 with the IRS Instructions

- Establish a Conflict of Interest Policy
- Establish financial management
  - o A corporate banking account,
  - o An accounting system adequate for
    - organizational management
    - tax reporting
    - grant tracking
    - proving substantiation letters to contibutors
  - o Meaningful financial oversight
  - o Internal controls
- Contact the state tax board for information about obtaining a state tax number and see if additional information must be submitted for state tax exemption from income tax and sales tax, etc.
- Check with the state department of consumer affairs or business licensing to obtain any required business licenses or permits.
- Contact the state Attorney General's Office to see if registration or reporting is required.
- Find out about workers' compensation if you will have employees.
- Protect your trade name
- Order any required notices (advertisements you

have to place) of your intent to begin operating in the community.

- Check zoning laws.
- Obtain city and/or county business licenses or permits.Get adequate insurance or a rider to a homeowner's policy.
- Get tax information for employees, including guidelines for withholding taxes, information on hiring independent contractors, etc.
- Apply for a federal non-profit mailing permit.
- Order business cards and stationery.
- Get an email address.
- Set up your website.
- Develop a Corporation Checklist of legal requirements for operation including:
    - o Board Meetings
    - o Tax Filings
    - o State Filings
- Ongoing steps to develop the organization
    - o Educate and Assess the Board
    - o Select, educate and evaluate the Director and key staff
    - o Develop a strategic plan
        - Review vision and mission
        - Review programs and activitics
        - Review financials, fundraising and legal compliance
        - Identify areas of growth and stagnation in the organization
        - Examine areas of possiblities for growth and needed services

6

NGO Perspectives on the Global Fund: A Report

> Such help as we can give each other in this world is a debt to each other; and the man who perceives a superiority or a capacity in a subordinate, and neither confesses nor assists it, is not merely the withholder of kindness, but the committer of injury.
>
> *—John Ruskin*

The Global Fund to Fight AIDS, Tuberculosis and Malaria (the Global Fund) was created in late 2001 to expand the response to the three diseases by raising new financial resources and disbursing these resources in countries in need. The Global Fund is designed to work through existing or new public-private partnerships at country level. In its first three rounds of funding, the Global Fund approved 227 proposals from 122 countries and three territories, involving expenditures of $2.1 billion 1 over two years. At its meeting on 28-30 June 2004, the Global Fund Board is scheduled to consider another $964 million in funding for proposals received in the fourth round.

After only a few years of operation, it is a little early to talk about the Global Fund's long-term impact.

Nevertheless, there have been some obvious successes. For example:

> The Global Fund has created a new model for doing business. Compared to bilateral and other multilateral funding programs, the Global Fund (a) is able to get money out more quickly; (b) is more creative and flexible; and (c) is more open and transparent with respect to its decision-making processes and information on approved projects. The Global Fund has focussed greater attention worldwide on HIV/AIDS, tuberculosis and malaria.
>
> In some countries, the Global Fund has brought new energy, team spirit and motivation to the fight against the three diseases. The Global Fund has raised some new resources. (It appears that not all of the resources raised by the Fund are new. It is difficult to know for sure, but it seems that some government donors to the Global Fund have simply re-channelled existing development assistance money.)

As well, through the establishment of Country Coordinating Mechanisms (CCMs), the Global Fund has affirmed and legitimatized the critical importance of the involvement of a full range of stakeholders in proposal development, implementation, monitoring and evaluation. Where the CCMs are working well, they provide unparalleled opportunities — often not available elsewhere — for the full range of stakeholders to work together in partnership. These stakeholders include governments, bilateral and multilateral donors, the private sector and civil society (including NGOs, affected communities and faith-based organizations).

The CCMs are working well in some countries. Unfortunately, however, this is not the case in most countries. This report documents some of the major concerns that NGOs have raised concerning the CCM process (see Section I).

This report also addresses other aspects of the Global Fund. The Fund is currently experiencing a serious shortfall in fundraising for future rounds of funding. This issue is discussed in Section II. As well, NGOs have identified concerns with respect to the Fund's governance and operations. These concerns are discussed in Section III.

In each of the three sections of this report, the description of the issues and concerns is followed by a list of the actions that ICASO believes need to be implemented to address these issues and concerns.

This report was compiled with input from the regional secretariats of ICASO and from representatives of HIV/AIDS NGOs actively working on Global Fund issues.

SECTION I: COUNTRY COORDINATING MECHANISMS

The following is a summary of the major concerns raised by NGOs related to the structure and operations of CCMs.

Issue No. 1

There is inadequate representation of NGOs and vulnerable populations — including women, persons living with the diseases, injection drug users and sex workers — on many CCMs

The composition of CCMs has been evolving over time, but it is evolving too slowly. While NGO representation on CCMs has increased since the first round of funding, it is still often inadequate. As a result, NGOs are under-represented on many CCMs in both quantity and quality. Also, people living with the diseases are still only marginally represented: There is still no representation of people living with the diseases in about 25 percent of the CCMs; on CCMs where there is representation from this sector, often it consists of only one person from one of the three disease communities. The purpose of involving people living with the diseases is often not well understood by the CCMs. As well, representation on many CCMs from other vulnerable populations is rare. For example, few CCMs have followed existing Global Fund guidelines on ensuring a gender balance. Furthermore, in many countries there is little representation on CCMs from civil society organizations located outside the capital city. Finally, in many countries there is no proper and transparent process for nominations to CCMs.

Issue No. 2

Civil society representatives have not been treated as full partners on many CCMs

Unfortunately, in many countries, despite having a seat at the table, civil society representatives have not played a significant role in deciding the content of proposals or in commenting on draft proposals. These are countries where the CCMs are dominated by government members who do not understand or appreciate the value of civil society involvement. In these countries, the government officials (and, in some cases bilateral and/or multilateral donors) control CCM member selection, meeting agendas and decision-making, however many civil society representatives sit on the CCM. In these countries, systems have not yet been established to allow for a participatory approach to decision-making. The problems described here tend to occur in countries where there is no culture of collaboration between governments and civil society, and where existing government structures do not allow for the full involvement of civil society under terms of equality and respect.

Issue No. 3

The roles and responsibilities of the members of CCMs and of the CCMs themselves are not clearly defined

On many CCMs, the roles of the individual members of the CCM have not been spelled out. Furthermore, the role of the CCM itself is not clear with respect to (a) the relationship to Principal Recipients (PRs), Sub-Recipients and Local Fund Agents; (b) the implementation of approved projects; and (c) the monitoring and evaluation of approved projects.

Issue No. 4

Many civil society representatives on CCMs do not have the skills they need to participate fully

Civil society representatives do not automatically come to the table with the knowledge and skills required to participate fully in policy-making; decision-making; priority-setting; and program design, implementation and monitoring. They often lack the skills to negotiate with other CCM members concerning their role on the CCM and their participation in CCM meetings. The financial and human resources required to expand the capacity of civil society representatives and improve their skills are often lacking.

Issue No. 5

The flow of information to and from CCMs, and within CCMs, is often inadequate

Three types of problems have been identified with respect to information sharing. First, problems of communication between CCM Secretariats and CCM members are widespread. Second, the flow of information from the Global Fund to CCMs is often quite limited. Third, communications from civil society representatives on the CCMs to members of their own constituencies have sometimes been deficient. The last problem is sometimes due to the limited communications infrastructures within many civil society organizations. In addition, the fact that many CCMs function in a grant-writing language that is not the first language of the country, or of some of the CCM members, limits civil society participation in these countries. Ineffective communication impedes participation.

Issue No. 6

Civil society representatives on some CCMs are not truly representative

In some countries, there is no adequate process in place to ensure that the civil society representatives on CCMs are truly able to represent the interests of their constituencies. In some cases, the problems stem from a flawed selection process that does not allow civil society organizations to choose their own representatives. In other cases, the problems are due to competition among NGOs. Another factor in some countries is the absence of representative national or umbrella NGO bodies.

Issue No. 7

The requirements of CCM participation contribute to a crisis in human and financial resource capacity among NGOs

The Global Fund is just one of many new and complex initiatives to which HIV/AIDS NGOs are expected to contribute time and energy. Unfortunately, the resources of these NGOs have not increased at the same rate as the increasing demands being placed on them.

ICASO Position

To address the concerns outlined above, related to the structure and operations of CCMs, ICASO calls for the following actions to be implemented:

> The Global Fund, in collaboration with civil society, should develop more detailed guidelines for CCMs. These guidelines should spell out minimum standards that CCMs have to meet. Specifically, the guidelines should: (a) define what constitutes adequate representation of NGOs and vulnerable populations; (b) set minimum requirements for the selections process; (c) define the roles and responsibilities of members of the CCMs; and (d) define the relationship of the CCM with respect to the PRs, Sub-Recipients and Local Fund Agents.
>
> Individual CCMs should develop terms of reference and operating procedures for the CCM. These terms of reference and operating procedures should define: (a) the composition of the CCM; (b) the selections process; (c) the roles and responsibilities of CCM members; and (d) the

relationship of the CCM with respect to the PRs, Sub-Recipients and Local Fund Agents.

The Global Fund should educate all members of CCMs (particularly government representatives) with respect to the importance of the participation on CCMs of NGOs, people living with the diseases, and other vulnerable populations.

Civil society delegations on the Global Fund Board, in consultation with their constituencies, should on an ongoing basis collectively formulate recommendations for ways in which civil society representation and participation on CCMs can be improved.

Individual CCMs should review the composition of their CCMs and take action to ensure that there is strengthened representation and meaningful participation from NGOs and vulnerable populations.

Civil society organizations should be funded to develop indicators to assess the effectiveness of civil society participation on CCMs, and to monitor the effectiveness of such participation. Either the Global Fund should directly fund civil society organizations to do this work, or it should facilitate a process that enables civil society organizations to obtain the necessary funding.

The Global Fund, in consultation with stakeholders, should monitor the governance and operations of CCMs on an ongoing basis, and should document and disseminate examples of good practice.

Technical assistance and resources should be provided to CCMs to enable them to (a) increase the capacity of civil society representatives (and other representatives, as required); (b) improve representation from outside the capital cities; (c) improve communications within CCMs, and from CCMs to the broader constituencies of CCM members; (d) allow CCMs to operate in more than one language, where required; (e) improve CCM governance; and (f) improve the operating efficiency of the CCMs. Either the Global Fund should invest in CCMs directly; or plans should be drawn up on a country-by-country basis to ensure that CCMs have coordinated and sustainable access to technical support and other resources.

Additional resources and technical assistance should be provided to HIV/AIDS NGOs to enable them to better respond to the increasing demands being placed on them by the need to participate in CCMs and other aspects of the Global Fund operations, and in other new initiatives. This support should be geared to increasing the management and coordination capacity of the NGOs to work in these environments. While this support does not necessarily have to come from Global Fund's own resources, the Fund should nevertheless play a facilitating role.

The Global Fund and other funders should provide more opportunities for the exchange of information among CCMs, including opportunities for inter-regional exchanges.

In those countries where competition among NGOs has raised concerns about the representativeness of the civil society representatives on the CCMs, individuals within these civil society organizations need to show leadership and take action to come up with a process to correct the problem.

SECTION II: FUNDING THE GLOBAL FUND

The Global Fund is facing a serious funding crisis. The Fund has stated that it needs to receive at least $1.4 billion in 2004 and $3.4 billion in 2005. The reason for the sharp increase in needs in 2005 is that the Fund has to start allocating funding not only for new projects but also for the final three years of the five-year projects approved in the early rounds of funding.

There is a growing concern among NGOs that the Global Fund is being overly conservative in its forecasts and that actual needs may be much higher.

As of 21 May 2004, total pledges were $1.5 billion for 2004 and $0.8 billion for 2005. Pledges for 2005 are only 26 percent of what the Global Fund says it needs, resulting in a current shortfall of $2.5 billion.

Many civil society organizations have proposed that the bulk of Global Fund revenues should come from the governments of the world's relatively affluent countries; and that the equitable contribution for each of these countries should be determined based on the country's gross national product (GNP). This approach is known as the Equitable Contribution Framework. (It should be noted that the Global Fund Board and many donor countries have not yet endorsed the Equitable Contribution Framework.)

President Jacques Chirac of France and others have proposed that the contributions to the Global Fund should be split into three equal parts, as follows: (a) the United States, which has 32.2 percent of world GNP, should pay one-third of the costs; (b) the European Union countries, which have 26.7 percent of world GNP, should pay one-third; and (c) other countries, which account for 41.1 percent of world GNP, should pay one-third.

Based on this formula, and using the Global Fund's own stated needs for 2004 and 2005, Aidspan 2 has calculated what the Equitable Contributions should be for each of the 41 countries defined by the World Bank as "high-income." Of these countries, 21 have not yet pledged anything for 2004 or 2005. These include Austria, Finland, Greece, Portugal, Switzerland and New Zealand. Among countries that have made pledges for these years, six have pledged less than their fair share for 2004 Australia, Canada, Iceland, Japan, South Korea and Singapore.

According to the Aidspan calculations, so far only two countries — France and the Netherlands — have pledged their fair share for 2005. All other high income countries have so far fallen short. To cite but a few examples:

> the United States has pledged $200 million for 2005, 18 percent of its Equitable Contribution of $1.1 billion;
>
> Japan has not pledged anything for 2005 (its Equitable Contribution would be $709 million);
>
> Germany has pledged $85 million for 2005, 35 percent of its Equitable Contribution of $242 million;
>
> Canada has pledged $52 million for 2005, 45

percent of its Equitable Contribution of $115 million;

the United Kingdom has pledged $58 million for 2005, 30 percent of its Equitable Contribution of $195 million; and

Australia has pledged $4 million for 2005, six percent of its Equitable Contribution of $63 million.

The shortfalls are even greater than what is shown above if one accepts that the Global Fund's own projected needs are too low. It is important to point out that the Equitable Contributions Framework represents minimum donations. If some countries donate amounts equal to the minimum, and some countries fall short, the Global Fund will never reach its fundraising goals.

ICASO Position

To address the funding crisis faced by the Global Fund, ICASO calls for the following actions to be implemented:

ICASO calls on all donor countries and the Global Fund Board to endorse the Equitable Contribution Framework.

ICASO calls on all donor countries that have not yet made contributions at least up to their Equitable Contributions for 2004 and 2005 to do so urgently.

Civil society organizations should increase and better coordinate their advocacy efforts to promote the Global Fund with the governments of donor countries.

SECTION III: GLOBAL FUND GOVERNANCE AND OPERATIONS

The following is a summary of the major concerns raised by NGOs concerning the governance and operations of the Global Fund.

Issue No. 1

People living with the diseases lack voice on the Global Fund Board. There are 18 voting positions and five ex-officio (non-voting) positions on the Global Fund board. Although there are two voting positions for NGO representatives, there is only one ex-officio position for a representative of the communities of people living with HIV/AIDS, tuberculosis or malaria.

Issue No. 2

The composition of most government delegations to the Global Fund Board does not adequately reflect public-private partnerships at country level. While two delegations — Italy and Latin America — have included civil society representation on their delegation, most delegations have no civil society members.

Issue No. 3

There have been problems getting money to NGOs who are implementing portions of approved projects. In some countries, PRs have been notoriously slow in moving Global Fund resources, particularly with respect to onward granting to NGOs. Often the PRs are governments, but many governments do not have adequate systems in place to award and track grants to NGOs. For example, in Zimbabwe, the NGOs are ready to begin implementing their portion of the approved Global Fund grant, and the Fund has provided the government with some of the grant monies, but the government has not yet provided the NGOs with the necessary funds.

Issue No. 4

There is a lack of clear criteria concerning the selection and role of PRs. The criteria for selecting PRs are not clear. As a result, there has been a lack of transparency in PR selection. The relationship of PRs to the CCMs is also unclear, and is potentially problematic in that the PRs are more accountable to the Global Fund Secretariat than to CCMs. Despite Global Fund guidance that requires that the PRs provide reports to the CCMs, few PRs are doing so.

Issue No. 5

There is a lack of coordination between the Global Fund and bilateral funding agencies. Although there is communication between the Global Fund and a range of bilateral funding agencies, this has not yet resulted in effective coordination of grant-making. Such coordination is crucial if approved projects are to operate efficiently and effectively.

Issue No. 6

The Global Fund has not created meaningful partnerships with civil society. Although the Global Fund has entered into formal partnership agreements with agencies such as the World Health Organization and UNAIDS, it has not yet done so with civil society organizations. Through formal partnerships with stable and well-resourced in-country NGOs, the Global Fund could fill some of the gaps that currently exist in the provision of technical support to these NGOs. UN agencies are generally not well positioned to provide this kind of support.

ICASO Position

To address the concerns outlined above, related to the governance and operations of the Global Fund, ICASO calls for the following actions to be implemented:

> The Global Fund should act immediately to ensure voting representation on the Global Fund Board for communities living with HIV/AIDS, tuberculosis and malaria.
>
> All government delegations to the Global Fund Board should include representation from NGOs and vulnerable populations. Resources need to be allocated to make this happen; the Global Fund can play a role in identifying appropriate sources of funding.
>
> Barriers to the flow of funds to NGOs that are implementing portions of approved Global Fund projects must be removed. To accomplish this, some or all of the following steps should be considered: (a) existing PRs should develop and implement as quickly as possible policies and procedures to allow for the timely flow of funds to NGOs; (b) training on the disbursement of funds should be provided for PRs, particularly where governments are acting as PRs; (c) the Global Fund should facilitate the sharing of good practices with respect to the flow of funds from governments to NGOs (e.g., the experiences of the government of Brazil); and (d) NGOs that are experienced in the disbursement of funds should be used as PRs. As well, in future rounds of funding, the criteria for the selection of PRs should include having the capacity to disburse funds to civil society organizations. The Global

Fund should develop detailed guidelines concerning the selection, roles and responsibilities of PRs. In particular, these guidelines should address the relationship of the PRs to the CCMs.

The Global Fund and bilateral funding agencies should coordinate their granting programs.

The Global Fund should enter into formal partnership agreements with civil society organizations, particularly international NGOs working on HIV/AIDS, tuberculosis and malaria.

Conclusion

As with any new organization, the Global Fund has endured its share of growing pains. As it evolves, it improves. ICASO believes that the Global Fund will continue to improve especially if civil society maintains strong advocacy efforts with the Board, the Secretariat and in-country.

The concerns described in this report need to be addressed soon if the Global Fund hopes to meet its goals and realize its potential. The building blocks for effective partnerships are in place at all levels of the Fund's operations and governance. But they need to be nurtured and bolstered before they can be fully effective.

The CCM process is a unique opportunity to develop partnerships in-country. The experience of the first few rounds of funding has demonstrated that CCMs work best in countries where civil society and governments are already working well together. Where these partnerships are not happening, where the CCMs are not operating effectively, the Global Fund has an obligation to step in to ensure that sufficient human, financial and technical resources are made available.

The Global Fund is no longer a new experiment. It's up, it's running. And it now needs to be based on a financing mechanism that is solid, predictable, reliable, and equitable. Donor governments need to view the Global Fund in the same way that they view their other national priorities, like contributions to international peacekeeping, or investments in domestic school systems. The Global Fund must be based on a truly joint and long-term global commitment to financing the war on AIDS, TB & malaria.

That commitment is what unites us. Much progress has been made to include a range of perspectives in the Global Fund's governance and its operations. But despite our best combined efforts, important voices remain marginalized and some partnerships are sadly superficial ones.

As this report has demonstrated, there is a lot of work to be done. And it needs to be done quickly.

With more and more implementation activities starting up, the possibilities for things to go awry are increasing. However, with strengthened partnerships, systems that run smoothly, representative governance, and realistic donor commitments, the Global Fund has the potential to alter the course of the epidemic. Civil society remains committed to helping the Global Fund to realize that potential, and we will do so by monitoring its progress and participating in its evolution.

KEY RESOURCES AND CONTACTS

Organizations and Individuals

The Global Fund to Fight HIV/AIDS, Tuberculosis and Malaria

Geneva Secretariat
53, Avenue Louis-Casaï
1216 Geneva-Cointrin, Switzerland
Tel: (41-22) 791 17 00
E-mail: info@theglobalfund.org
Website: http://www.theglobalfund.org/en/

Vacant
Civil Society Relations Manager
Tel: (41-22) 791 1767

Doris D' Cruz-Grote
Coordinator, CCM Development
Tel: (41-22) 791 1790
E-mail: doris.dcruzgrote@theglobalfund.org

NGO and Community Global Fund Board Members, Alternates and Communication Focal Points

Developing Country NGO Representatives
REPRESENTATIVE
Rita Arauz Molina
President, Nimehuatzin Foundation
Nicaragua
Tel: (50-52) 278 0028
E-mail: nimehuatzin@cablenet.com.ni

ALTERNATE
Razia Essack-Kauaria
Secretary General, Namibia Red Cross Society
Tel: (264-61) 23 5226
E-mail: secgen@redcross.org.na

COMMUNICATION FOCAL POINT
Lucy Ng'ang'a
Executive Director
Tanzania
Eastern African National Networks of AIDS Service Organizations
Tel: (255-27) 250 7521
E-mail: eannasop@eannaso.org

Developed Country NGO Representatives
REPRESENTATIVE
Hélène Rossert-Blavier
Director General, AIDES, France
Tel: (33-1) 4183 4606
E-mail: hrossert@aides.org

ALTERNATE
Jairo Pedraza
Director, International Programs
Cicatelli Associates Inc., USA
Tel: (1-212) 594-7741 ext. 242
E-mail: jpgfna@aol.com

COMMUNICATION FOCAL POINT
Richard Burzynski
Executive Director
ICASO, Canada
Tel: (1-416) 921-0018 ext.15
E-mail: richardb@icaso.org

Communities Living with the Diseases Representatives
REPRESENTATIVE
Anandi Yuvaraj
Program Officer, India HIV/AIDS Alliance
Tel: (91-11) 51633 081
E-mail: ayuvaraj@allianceindia.org

ALTERNATE
Rodrigo Pascal
Executive Coordinator, Vivo Positivo
REDLA+, Chile
Tel: (56-2) 635 9396
E-mail: rpascal@vivopositivo.org

COMMUNICATION FOCAL POINT
Stuart Flavell
Executive Director
Global Network of People Living with HIV/AIDS (GNP+)
The Netherlands
Tel: (31-20) 423 4114
E-mail infognp@gnpplus.net

Other Organizations

Aidspan
Website: www.aidspan.org

Fund-the-Fund Campaign
Website: www.fundthefund.org

7

NGO Participation in National AIDS Control Program: Basic Guidelines

HIV/AIDS in India is a serious public health challenge which has certain socioeconomic dimensions. The strategy of the National AIDS Control Project - II is to formulate a multi-sectoral response that will integrate the concerns of HIV/AIDS into the larger development effort both in the Government and voluntary sector. It is also critical, in any program to control HIV/AIDS, to reach the most vulnerable and marginalized communities with focused counseling and services to enable them to change their behavior. These populations can best be reached through Non Government Organization (NGO's) and Community Based Organizations (CBO's) who have credible track records and connectivity with the community. The NACP - II envisages NGOs as critical partners for targeted interventions, voluntary testing and counseling and school AIDS education activities. NGOs and CBOs are also being involved in care and outreach services for people living with HIV/AIDS.

A transparent and viable process is critical to ensure that NGOs with skills, credibility and relevant experience are selected to participate in the State and National Program.

NACO has developed detailed guidelines for selection, capacity building, funding and monitoring of NGOs. These guidelines have been approved by the World Bank and the National AIDS Control Board.

1. Appoint an NGO Advisor Through an Open and Transparent System

An advertisement must be issued in the local newspapers for the post of NGO Advisor. A selection committee should select the NGO advisor. It is mandatory that a representative from NACO is a member of the selection committee.

The NGO Advisor should have a Masters degree in Social Work or any other social science discipline such as Sociology, Anthropology etc. The age of the NGO Advisor should be between 25-50 years. He/she should have at least two years experience in the NGO sector preferably in the health sector. Past experience in the HIV/AIDS field would be an added advantage. The advisor should possess excellent communication skills both written and verbal and knowledge of local language. The position is purely temporary and on contract basis. The initial placement is for one year, extendable for another year based on performance. (The details on the qualifications and terms of reference of the NGO Advisor are at Annexure - I).

2. Prominent NGOs would be appointed as members of the Executive Committee of State AIDS Control Society.

3. Selecting NGOs

An advertisement must be issued in the newspapers to invite proposals from NGOs. (A copy of the advertisement is at Annexure-II).

4. Assessment of the NGO

The NGOs, which have sent an application, should be assessed on the following guidelines:

4.1 Registration Detials

Legal Status: The NGO should be a legally registered Organization, including:

- Organization registered under the Societies Registration Act of 1860,
- Charitable companies registered under the Charitable and Religion Act 1920;
- Public Trusts registered under the Indian Trust Act, 1982;
- Cooperatives professional bodies such as IIPA, IMA
- The NGO should be registered for period of minimum three years.

4.2 Infrastructure

The basic infrastructure of the NGO should be in place (premises, basic office equipment, basic teaching aids). At times the NGO Advisor may have to physically verify this.

4.3 Stable Organizational Structure

(which can help to ensure accountability). This will include staff structure/number, name/roles & responsibilities of the staff involved in the project, organization's capabilities, staff experience and expertise in context of program/project, geographical area covered by the organization, other projects undertaken by the Organization.

4.4 NGOs Having Strong Credible Links Should be Given Reference

While shortlisted give preference to NGOs having established track record in any other development field such as welfare, it women, working with marginalized groups such as commercial sex workers, street children, intravenous drug users, and slum community. Active involvement of the NGOs on any of the above areas is desirable. This would be one of the ways to ensure that the NGO has established strong credible links with the community and may effectively integrate HIV/AIDS with its ongoing Program.

4.5 A True and Fair Track Record in Terms of the Financial Side of Its Operations

This would necessarily involve having clean audit reports relating to its past activities.

The NGO should not have been blacklisted by the Central Social Welfare Board (CSWB) and Council for Advancement of People's Action and Rural Technology (CAPART) or any other Government agency.

4.6. Good Working Relationship and Networking with Other NGOs

Government bodies (in the NGO's operational area).

5. Documents

The Project proposal should be accompanied with the following documents:

- Copy of the registration certificate
- Annual report of the past three years.
- Non- Governmental Organization's Self Assessment Report
- Audited financial report of the past three years.
- Organogram of the NGO

Certificate from the NGO stating that it is not receiving funds for the activity mentioned in the proposal from any other national or international donor agencies or State Government.

6. Scruitininzing Applications Received from NGOs

6.1 All the proposals received from the NGOs would be placed before a Technical Advisory Committee (TAC), consisting of technical advisors of the State AIDS Control Societies and the NGO members of the Executive Committee of the State AIDS Control Societies. Wherever possible, a member of NACO would also be part of the selection committee. The NGO Advisor would be the convener of the Technical Advisory Committee.

The Technical Advisory Committee would meet every month for about two or three days, to review the progress of the NGO support programme.

6.2 The Financial Advisory Committee: would scrutinize the proposals with reference to the priority-targeted intervention identified for the State/MC in its final Project Implementation Plan. Proposals would be taken up in the chronological order of receipt in the SACS.

6.3 After the scrutiny, the TECHNICAL ADVISORY COMMITTEE may come to one of the following four recommendations:

- Approve the proposal in to to and recommend it for field inspection.
- Recommend modification of the proposal in terms of the budget
- Recommend modification of the proposal in terms of the strategies adopted
- Reject the proposal, after recording the specific reasons.

Those NGOs whose proposals were recommended by the TECHNICAL ADVISORY COMMITTEE for modification would be informed of the decision and they would be invited to participate in a short Orientation Training Program (OTP). This Orientation Training Program will train the NGOs in understanding the principles of Targeted interventions and formulating viable proposals according to the guidelines. The TECHNICAL ADVISORY COMMITTEE will consider the modified proposal once it is received, in its chronological order, as per the normal procedure.

6.4 The proposals approved in to to will be taken up for field inspection by a Joint Appraisal Team (JAT) consisting of an officer of SACS who has been designated as Zonal Officer for specific districts and one of the NGO members of TECHNICAL ADVISORY COMMITTEE. The Joint Appraisal Team will also take efforts to find out the credibility of the NGO in the local community. The field inspection report of the Joint Appraisal Team, along with the Technical Advisory Committee's recommendations, will be placed before the next meeting of the Executive Committee of SACS, chaired by the State Health Secretary, for consideration and a decision.

6.5 Those NGOs whose proposals were rejected by the TECHNICAL ADVISORY COMMITTEE, Joint Appraisal Team or the EC will be informed in writing stating briefly the reasons for rejection.

7. Project Proposal

Those NGOs whose proposals were recommended by the TECHNICAL ADVISORY COMMITTEE for modification would be informed of the decision and they would be invited to participate in a short Orientation

Training Program (OTP). This OTP will train the NGOs in understanding the principles of Targeted interventions and formulating viable proposals according to the core principals of targeted interventions which are as follows:

1. Behavior Change Communication
2. Condom Programming
3. STD Awareness and Counseling
4. Creating an Enabling Environment.

7.1 Application Profile

On the basis of the self assessment provided by the NGO and the stated objectives, the proposal should briefly comment on the infrastructure, personnel, financial capabilities and the programs/activities being implemented by the Organization.

7.2 Project Objectives

The proposal must clearly specify the needs of the project. They should be appropriate to the scale and the nature of the problem it seeks to address. The project activities should be consistent with the priorities in the strategic plan and the NACP plan. The project should integrate HIV/AIDS with its ongoing activities.

7.3 Project Context

The proposal must indicate that the applicant NGO is aware, and knowledgeable of the HIV/AIDS situation in the identified geographical area, where it wishes to implement the project. The proposal must take into account the existing or potential constraints that might impede the development of the project.

7.4 Personnel

The personnel listed in the proposal should be in accordance with the project activities. For example a proposal on counseling should have two counselors and one project coordinator. Similarly a proposal on awareness generation should have a project coordinator and peer educators. The emphasis should be on integrating the HIV/AIDS Program with the NGO's existing programs. To achieve this wherever possible, qualified personnel already on the rolls of the NGO should be given an honorarium to carry on the project activities.

7.5 Work Plan

The work plan should be clear and doable and have potential for achieving the project objectives. There should be scope for participation by the target group community in planning, implementing and evaluating the project. The proposal should have a calendar of activities for each month.

7.6 Project Output

The proposal specify clear, qualitative and quantitative outputs, which are consistent with the project objectives?

7.7. Monitoring and Evaluation

The proposal should be include a system for project monitoring and reviews. The planned evaluation methodology should be consistent with the objectives and scale of the project.

7.8 Sustainbility

The project should be able to serve as a replaceable example to NGOs and the others active in the field of

AIDS. The project should be in a position to mobilize funds from alternate sources over a period of time or be able to scale down its funding needs through successive years. The project should be able to integrate HIV/AIDS activities with its ongoing activities.

7.9 Budget

The budget lines should be clearly laid out. The overall financial expenditure proposed should be reasonable, adequate to carry out specified activities, and the role of each staff projected in the budget justified. It should conform to the budget guidelines given by NACO with a flexibility 10 - 15%.

There should be a general embargo on buying vehicles and construction of buildings. Any equipment purchased under the project such as computers, telephone etc. should be a property of the State AIDS Society.

7. 10 Release of Fund

NGOs whose proposals are approved by the Eexecutive Committee will enter into an agreement with the SACS and thereafter the funds will be disbursed to the NGOs on the basis of the following pattern

> For Targeted Interventions Administrative approval should be given for period of 3 years and financial sanction given for the current year based on the approved budget.
>
> The contribution of the NGO can be in terms of infrastructure staff or in kind. The SACs should release 100% sanctioned budget to the NGO as per NACO Guidelines.
>
> The amount sanctioned should be disbursed in

two six monthly installments. The first installment would comprise the entire non-recurring expenditure of the project plus 50% recurring expenditure for the first six months.

The Second instalment would comprise of the balance recurring expenditure that is 50 % of the recurring expenditure. Any unspent balance is to be carried forward in the second year.

The second installment would be sanctioned after receiving a progress report and an unaudited statement of expenditure from the Organisation.

The Organisation would be required to submit a full project report, audited annual statement of accounts and utilization certificate within one month from the date of completion of the project.

Before funds are released, the NGO is required to submit an inception report as per the format placed at Annexure I.

The NGO contribution of 10% of the budget may be calculated in terms of the infrastructure, human resources and any other assets which would be utilised for project activity. This would be in addition to the 100% funds sanctioned.

In addition to the inception report the NGO is required to submit a Bond (Annexure II.)

The fund released to the NGO is an activity grant and does not require to be backed by an bank guarantee.

The organization is to submit monthly reports as devised under the Monitoring & Evaluation system.

ANNEXURE I

INCEPTION REPORT

1. Name of the Organisation.
   - i. Address;
     - a. Postal
     - b. E-mail
   - ii. Telephone/Fax No.
   - iii. Legal Status #iv. Registration Number
     v.Registration Date.
   - vi. Name of the Project.
   - vi. Duration of the Project
   - vii. Area to be covered
   - ix. Target Groups
     - a. Category
     - b. Target population to be covered
     - c. Budget:
       Proposed
2. Infrastructure:
   - a. Land, Building
   - b. Basic Office Equipment
   - c. Fixed Assets
   - d. Moveable Assets
3. Organisation Structure
   No. of Supervisory & Support Staff
   Experties/ Capabilities & Experience of the Management

4. Liabilities

   Grant received from any International/National Donor

   Agencies or State Government

   Name of Agency

5. Nature of the Project

   Quantum of Grant

   Bank

6. Name & Branch

   Account No.

   Authorised Signatories.

ANNEXURE-II

NATIONAL AIDS CONTROL ORGANIZATION

Qualifications:	Masters degree in Social Work or any other Social Science discipline such as sociology, anthropology etc.
Experience :	At least two years experience in working in the NGO sector preferably in the health sector. Past experience in the HIV/AIDS field would be an added advantage. - Excellent communication skills. - Knowledge of local language.
Age :	25 to 50 Years
Salary:	Consolidated pay of RS. 10,000/- per month. The salary would be drawn from the NGO budget for AIDS control and prevention Program.
Placement:	The headquarters of the NGO Advisor would be the State AIDS Cell.
Reporting:	He/She would be reporting to the Project Director, State AIDS Control Society
Position :	The position is purely temporary and on contract basis . The initial contract is for one year, extendable for another year based On Applications are invited from interested voluntary organization in the state/UT of for implementing AIDS awareness and control program.

NGOs interested in HIV/AIDS work may send in a proposal on (I) generating awareness, (ii) intervention programs

Tenure : performance.The appointment of NGO Advisor would be through an open and transparent system of advertisement in the leading newspapers of the state.

Role & Responsibility:

1. Adopt the National program strategy for the involvement of NGOs based on an assessment of priority needs and in keeping with the broad framework of the National AIDS Control Program.

2. Assess the strengths and weaknesses of the NGOs that are addressing health and development issues through their current program to examine the potential of involving them in AIDS Control activities. Encourage the involvement of those that have such potential by sensitizing them to the problems and assisting them in identifying program activities that match their specific interests and expertise.

3. Encourage and stimulate the development of new NGOs to respond to the AIDS crisis and to help develop the capacity of these organizations to address various social, legal, ethical and other dimensions of the problem.

4. To scrutinize the project proposals in the light of the,"Guidelines for NGO Assistance", and recommended to the Project Director for approval of the Executive Committee of the SACS.

5. To communicate the decision of the AIDS Cell of State/ UT Government to the NGOs.

6. To assist the NGOs in the implementation of the project.

7. Organize technical and managerial backup mechanisms either directly and or through intermediary organisation to assist individual NGO in programme planning, including proposal writing as well as for providing subsequent inputs for programme development, monitoring and evaluation based on needs and demands of individual NGOs.

8. Identify intermediary NGOs that could serve as networking and support institutions for clusters of Ngos that are working in the specific geographic locations and/or in particular programmatic areas of concern.

9. To act as liaison officer between the Govt., NGOs and other agencies in the State/UT.

10. Any other work as may be assigned to him/her by the State AIDS Program Officer/ Program Coordinator/ Director of Health services/ Secretary, Health

	& Family Welfare Department/ Chief Secretary of the State /UT.
Monitoring & Travel Terms:	The Advisor will have to travel extensively in the state for&field level monitoring and will be provided staff vehicle or I St. class railway fare and TA/DA as per Government rules.
Disputes:	In case of any disputes about job assigned and work report appraisal the decision of the Health Secretary would be Final in the matter.

8

Starting Nonprofit Organization in US and Relevant Issues

> Zeal without knowledge is like fire without a grate to contain it; like a sword without a hilt to wield it by; like a high-bred horse without a bridle to guide him. It speaks without thinking, acts without planning, seeks to accomplish a good end without the adoption of becoming mean.
>
> —*Julius Bate*

I

Have you always wanted to leave the world a better place than you found it by starting a nonprofit corporation? Here's a simple, straightforward guide on how to successfully establish a 501(c)(3) nonprofit corporation.

Steps

1. Understand what a nonprofit is: an organization whose primary objective is to support some issue or matter of private interest or public concern (such as the arts, charities, education, politics, religion, research, or some other endeavor) for non-commercial purposes. There are different kinds of nonprofits, one of them being a 501(c)(3), which is exempt from income and (sometimes) property tax,

and able to receive tax-deductible charitable contributions.

2. Formulate a mission statement. As a non-profit organization, you exist to accomplish your mission, which should be crafted based upon your purpose, services and values. The mission statement is a concise expression that covers in one or two sentences who the organization is, what it does, for whom and where. It should also be compelling, as it will be used in all published materials, funding requests and public relations. It should also portray how your organization is distinct from others.
3. Form a Board of Directors. Forming a board requires careful thought and extensive recruitment efforts. Each state has regulations that determine the minimum size of the board, typically three, but the optimum number of people who sit on the board should be determined by the needs of the organization. Based on what your organization would like to accomplish, you should decide what special skills and qualities you will require of the individuals on your board. Identify qualified individuals who are supportive of your mission and are willing to give of their talents and time.
4. File Articles of Incorporation. Articles of Incorporation are official statements of creation of an organization filed with the appropriate state agency. They are important to protect both board and staff from legal liabilities incurred by the organization, making the corporation the holder of debts and liabilities, not the individuals and officers who work for the organization. The specific requirements governing how to incorporate are

determined by each state. You can obtain the information you need to proceed with this step from your state Attorney General's office or your state Secretary's office.

5. Draft bylaws. Bylaws are simply the "rules" of how the organization operates. Although Bylaws are not required to file for 501(c)(3) status, they will help you in governing your organization. Bylaws should be drafted with the help of an attorney and approved by the board early in the organization's development.
6. Develop a budget. Creating a budget is often one of the most challenging tasks when creating a nonprofit organization. A budget is the expression, in financial terms, of the plan of operation designed to achieve the objectives of an organization. New organizations may start the budgeting process by looking at potential income – figuring out how much money they have to spend.
7. Develop a record-keeping system. Legally, you must save all Board documents including minutes and financial statements. It is necessary to preserve your important corporate documents, including board meeting minutes, bylaws, Articles of Incorporation, financial reports, and other official records. You should contact your appropriate state agency for more information on what records you are required to keep in the official files.
8. Develop an accounting system. If your board does not include someone with a financial or accounting background, it is best to work with an accountant familiar with non-profit organizations. Nonprofits are accountable to the public, their funders, and,

in some instances, government granting bodies, and it is vital to establish a system of controls (checks and balances) when establishing the organization's accounting practices. Responsible financial management requires the establishment of an accounting system that meets both current and anticipated needs.

9. File for 501(c)(3) status. To apply for recognition of tax-exempt, public charity status, obtain Form 1023 (application) and Publication 557 (detailed instructions) from the local IRS office. The filing fee depends upon the size of the organization's budget. The application is an important legal document, so it is advisable to seek the assistance of an experienced attorney when preparing it.
10. Apply for a federal employer identification number. Regardless of whether or not you have employees, nonprofits are required to obtain a federal Employer Identification Number (EIN) — also referred to as the federal ID number. Available from the IRS, this number is used to identify the organization when tax documents are filed and is used not unlike an individual's Social Security number. If you received your number prior to incorporation, you will need to apply for a new number under the corporate name. Ask for Form SS-4 when applying for your EIN.
11. File for state and local tax exemption. In accordance with state, county, and municipal law, you may apply for exemption from income, sales, and property taxes. Contact your state Department of Revenue, your county or municipal Department of Revenue, local Departments of Revenue, and county or municipal clerk's offices.

12. Fulfill charitable solicitation law requirements. If your organization's plans include fundraising, be aware that many states and few local jurisdictions regulate organizations that solicit funds within that state, county, or city. Usually compliance involves obtaining a permit or license and then filing an annual report and financial statement. Contact the state Attorney General's office, the state Department of Commerce, state and local Departments of Revenue and county or municipal clerk's offices to get more information.
13. Apply for a nonprofit mailing permit. The federal government provides further subsidies for nonprofits with reduced postage rates on bulk mailings. While first-class postage rates for nonprofits remain the same as those for the for-profit sector, second- and third-class rates are substantially less when nonprofits mail to a large number of members or constituencies. For more information on eligibility, contact the U.S. Postal Service and ask for Publication 417, Nonprofit Standard Mail Eligibility

Tips

- Sample mission statement: "The National Mental Health Association is dedicated to promoting mental health, preventing mental disorders and achieving victory over mental illnesses through advocacy, education, research and service; The National Consumer Supporter Technical Assistance Center's purpose is to strengthen consumer organizations by providing technical assistance in the forms of research, informational materials, and financial aid. The mission of Texas Mental Health Consumers is to organize, encourage, and educate mental health consumers in Texas. TMHC supports and promotes the mental health recovery process through peer directed and operated services, advocacy, economic development, and participation in public mental health policy design."

- What to look for in a board member: Look for individuals whose values reflect your statement of purpose. Although it is recommended that the majority of your board be consumers, include the community at large, not just your specific community of focus (e.g. the mental health community). Consider the religious community, local service clubs, legal professionals, and colleges and universities as sources for prospective a Board of Directors. Do not overload people who already serve on many committees – seek a balance between old and new leadership.
- The organization needs to open a bank account and ascertain whether to use the accrual or cash method of accounting. The difference between the two types of accounting is when revenues and expenses are recorded. In cash basis accounting, revenues are recorded when cash is actually received and expenses are recorded when they are actually paid (no matter when they were actually invoiced). In accrual basis accounting, income is reported in the fiscal period it is earned, regardless of when it is received, and expenses are deducted in the fiscal period they are incurred, whether they are paid or not.
- Hire an attorney to help you with your Certificate of Incorporation and the By-Laws. Hire an attorney or accountant, particularly one who has experience

with 501c3 nonprofit corporations, to help you file the state and federal exemption forms. It will save you time and money in the long run.

Warnings

- Do not use an Incorporation service or Paralegal document processing service to start your nonprofit. They often only provide part of your documentation needed for full Tax Exempt Corporation status. Consult a nonprofit law attorney, an experienced accountant or a professional 501(c)(3) consulting service, but be sure to check them out. Most paralegals, attorneys and accountants have little experience in this area. You can usually check out these services via the local legal bar association, references, or the Better Business Bureau (though the BBB charges businesses hundreds of dollars to list with them).
- It is important to file your 1023 within 27 months of the date when your organization was established, or when your Articles of Incorporation were filed. Although the IRS may approve an additional extension under certain circumstances, missing the deadline may result in your charity or foundation not getting 501(c)(3) recognition retroactive to its incorporation date.

II

WORLD VISION: A CASE STUDY

World Vision, founded in the United States in 1950, is an international Christian relief and development organization whose stated goal is "working for the well being of all people, especially children." Working on six continents,

World Vision is one of the largest Christian relief and development organisations in the world with $1B budget (2005).

World Vision is a Christian relief and development organization dedicated to helping children and their communities worldwide reach their full potential by tackling the causes of poverty. The organization was started in 1950 by Dr. Bob Pierce, a young Christian minister, in China and then South Korea. Dr. Pierce, associated with the Youth for Christ organization, felt compassion for the children in his ministry.

World Vision began caring for orphans and other children in need throughout Asia and then eventually in more than 90 countries, embracing larger issues of community development and advocacy for the poor as part of its basic mission to help children and their families build a sustainable future. In 2005, World Vision's work by more than 20,000 staff across the globe affected the lives of 100 million people worldwide, including 1.85 million in the United States. Five million donors, supporters and volunteers helped the organization to achieve its goals.

World Vision's organizational structure operates as a federation of interdependent national offices, each overseen by their own boards or advisory councils. A common mission statement and shared core values bind the partnership offices and members together. Each partner abides by common policies and standards and holds each other a through an ongoing system of peer review. The partnership offices – located in Geneva, Bangkok, Nairobi, Cyprus, Los Angeles, and San José – coordinate strategic operations of the organization and represent World Vision in the international arena. Each national office enjoys an equal voice in the organization's governance, erasing traditional distinctions between the developed and developing world.

An international board of directors oversees the World Vision Partnership. The full board meets twice a year to appoint senior officers, approve strategic plans and budgets, and determine international policy.

The chairperson of the international board is Denis St. Armour of Canada. The international president and chief executive officer is Dr. Dean R. Hirsch.

Funding

About 80% of World Vision's funding comes from private sources, including individuals, World Vision clubs in schools such as the Taipei American School, corporations, and foundations. The remainder comes from governments and multilateral agencies. Aside from cash contributions, World Vision accepts gifts in kind, typically food commodities, medicine, and clothing donated through corporations and government agencies.

Approximately half of World Vision's programs are funded through child sponsorship. Individuals, families, churches, and other groups sponsor specific children or specific community projects in their own country or abroad. Sponsors send funds each month to provide support for the sponsored children or projects.

In 2005, 87% of funding went to programs, 8% went to fundraising and 5% went to management & general. World Vision has announced a goal of reducing the fundraising + management & general "overhead" to 10% from 13% currently. Thanks to gifts in kind and grants, one dollar invested by individual donors results in $1.50 in program funding.

Activities

World Vision aims to contribute to people's needs in five major areas; emergency relief, education, health care, economic development, and promotion of justice. World Vision activities include transformational development, emergency relief, strategic initiatives, public awareness campaigns and promoting Christianity.

Transformational development occurs through focusing on improvement of children's lives. This process first helps people and their communities recognize the resources that lie within themselves to make change possible. With support from World Vision, communities transform themselves by carrying out their own development projects in health care, agriculture production, water projects, education, micro-enterprise development, advocacy and other community programs.

World Vision provides *emergency relief* to people whose lives are endangered by disasters or conflict and who need immediate, skilled assistance. World Vision attempts to respond to all major emergencies around the world themselves or in cooperation with their partner agencies. For example, World Vision has responded to famine in Ethiopia and North Korea, hurricanes in Central America, the tsunami in the Indian Ocean nations, earthquakes in El Salvador, India, Taiwan and Turkey, and war refugees in Kosovo, Chechnya, Sierra Leone, Angola, and East Timor.

World Vision also addresses the complex, systematic factors that perpetuate poverty by *promoting justice*. World Vision supports community awareness of the collective ability to address unjust practices and begin working for change. World Vision speaks out on issues such as child labor, debt relief for poor nations, and the use of children as combatants in armed conflict. World Vision International has endorsed the Universal Declaration of Human Rights and the United Nations Convention on the Rights of the Child as fundamental expressions of the freedoms and responsibilities that should exist in every country. World Vision fosters opportunities to help reduce conflict levels and to contribute to the peaceful resolution of hostilities and reconciliation of disputes.

As a Christian organization, World Vision participates in *strategic initiatives* with Christian leaders and lay people of all denominations through conferences, consultations, training programmes and various educational opportunities. World Vision is an ecumenical organization willing to partner with all Christian churches. Yet, World Vision is respectful of other faiths.

World Vision encourages *public awareness* about the needs of others, the causes of poverty, and the nature of compassionate response. These efforts include collaboration with media and community participation in fundraising. In all its communications, World Vision upholds the dignity of suffering children and families in presenting explanations of the causes and consequences of poverty, war, neglect, and abuse.

World Vision believes *witnessing for Christ* is a fundamental part of their relief work. The organization believes that God, in the person of Jesus, offers hope of renewal, restoration, and reconciliation. World Vision seeks to express this message through "life, deed, word, and sign". World Vision's programs and services are provided without regard to race, ethnic origin, gender, or religion. All of its US staff are required to sign a statement affirming their belief in Jesus Christ, and background checks are often made with an individual's pastor or priest. However, employees of subcontractors or World Vision partners are not required to have any Christian affiliation. World Vision offices in predominantly non-Christian countries do hire staff of other faiths, and in some countries even the majority of staff may be non-Christians in sympathy with World Vision's ethos and objectives.

In 2004, World Vision was active in the following countries:

Africa

Angola, Burundi, Chad, Democratic Republic of Congo, Ethiopia, Ghana, Kenya, Lesotho, Liberia, Malawi, Mali, Mauritania, Mozambique, Niger, Rwanda, Senegal, Sierra Leone, Somalia, South Africa, Sudan, Swaziland, Tanzania, Uganda, Zambia, Zimbabwe.

Asia and The Pacific

Afghanistan, Australia, Bangladesh, Cambodia, People's Republic of China (Mainland and Hong Kong) , East Timor, India, Indonesia, Japan, Laos, Malaysia, Mongolia, Myanmar, Nepal, New Zealand, North Korea, Pakistan, Papua New Guinea, Philippines, Singapore, Solomon Islands, South Korea, Sri Lanka, Republic of China (Taiwan), Thailand, Uzbekistan, Vanuatu, Vietnam.

Europe and the Middle East

Albania, Armenia, Austria, Azerbaijan, Bosnia and Herzegovina, Finland, France, Georgia, Germany, Ireland, Israel, Lebanon, Macedonia, Montenegro, Netherlands, Romania, Russia, Serbia, Spain, Switzerland, Syria, United Arab Emirates, United Kingdom.

Latin America

Argentina, Bolivia, Brazil, Chile, Colombia, Costa Rica, Dominican Republic, Ecuador, El Salvador, Guatemala, Haiti, Honduras, Mexico, Nicaragua, Peru.

North America

Canada, United States of America.

Appendices

APPENDIX—1

UNEP POLICY ON NGOS AND OTHER MAJOR GROUPS

1. Background

The 1992 United Nations Conference on Environment and Development (UNCED) identified as partners for governments and the international system key sectors in society, henceforth referred to as Major Groups. UNCED's Agenda 21, noting the need for new forms of participation and addressing the means for moving towards real social partnership in support of common efforts for sustainable development, mentions as Major Groups women, children and youth, indigenous people, farmers, local authorities, business and industry, the scientific and technological community, workers and trade unions, and non-governmental organizations. In Chapter 28, Agenda 21 calls on UNEP to raise "general awareness and action in the area of environmental protection through collaboration with the general public, non-governmental entities and intergovernmental institutions".

Prior to UNCED, the 1972 Stockholm Conference on the Human Environment that led to the founding of UNEP saw an unprecedented role being played by NGOs in shaping the international environmental agenda. In Resolution 2997

(XXVII) of 15 December 1972 (paragraph IV.5), which established UNEP, the United Nations General Assembly invited, "those non-governmental organizations that have an interest in the field of the environment to lend their full support and collaboration to the United Nations with a view to achieving the largest possible degree of cooperation".

The Stockholm Action Plan, in Recommendation 97, stated that, "the programme must provide means of stimulating active participation by the citizens, and of eliciting interest and contributions from non-governmental organizations for the preservation and development of the environment".

Successive UNEP Governing Council resolutions have re-emphasized the need for working with the widest possible range of public organizations, notably GC.16/7 ("Volunteers for the Environment") of 1991. GC.18/4 ("The role of non-governmental organizations in UNEP") of 1995 calls on UNEP to develop a policy framework and appropriate mechanisms for working with NGOs.

2. Objectives

The purpose of this document is to review collaboration with the non-governmental sector(s) in the context of a new and integrated approach to programme planning and the new trends for engaging civil society since UNCED and the emergence of the Commission on Sustainable Development (CSD).

NGOs and other Major Groups are key stakeholders, directly or indirectly, on most environmental issues and relevant solutions. NGOs have the added importance of being the organizational form used by the other categories of Major Groups. They and other organized manifestations of Major Groups such as scientific and professional associations, service clubs, community-based organizations (CBOs) and grassroots organizations (GROs), consumer unions and Environmental Citizen's Organizations (ECOs) are of critical importance as:

- actual and potential partners in programme and project planning, implementation and evaluation;
- cost-effective channels for disseminating environmental information and for bringing to UNEP's attention evolving issues and perspectives in civil society;
- front line innovators in many fields who have expertise to offer in a wide range of disciplines;
- mobilizers of local resources and capacity for problem-solving critical for sustainable development; and, increasingly;
- key allies in advocacy, an independent voice calling for changes in ethics and values, urging the United Nations system and Governments to rationalize global cooperation, avoid duplication, waste and misapplication of resources.

3. UNEP Collaboration with NGOs and other Major Groups

UNEP and the non-governmental sector(s) stand to benefit from continued and increased collaboration. In this partnership, UNEP shall:

i) institutionalize NGO/Major Groups participation in project design, implementation and evaluation;

ii) continually review mechanisms for cooperation with NGOs/Major Groups with a view to keeping abreast with global and regional trends and needs to the best of its ability;

iii) encourage and, where feasible, support the participation of NGOs/Major Groups in policy development and governance of the organization, bringing to the attention of Governing Council proposals for broader participation and access whenever necessary;

iv) co-fundraise with individual NGO/Major Groups partners to finance agreed projects and programmes.

4. Responsibilities.

i) UNEP Headquarters

UNEP Headquarters is responsible for guiding, coordinating, catalyzing and as far as global environmental problems are concerned, operationalizing collaboration with the non-governmental sector(s). In general, UNEP HQ shall:

a) through the Assistant Executive Director for the Policy and External Affairs Division provide policy guidance on, promote and see to NGO/Major Groups participation in Governing Council sessions;

b) maintain NGO databases and background information on global developments relating to NGOs/Major Groups, including information on participation in programme implementation and significant policy inputs;

c) through the Information and Public Affairs Branch develop outreach strategies for involving NGOs/ Major Groups and other constituencies in UNEP's work and for backing their own initiatives, ensure information exchange between UNEP and the NGOs/ Major Groups and collaborative programmes in this regard, facilitate day-to-day access of NGOs/ Major Groups to different programme units, arrange meetings and policy briefings with top management, and accreditation for Governing Council and other meetings.

d) through the substantive units involve NGOs and other Major Group stakeholder organizations in the design and implementation of UNEP's work programme according to their competence and relevance;

e) give assistance to and liaise with Regional and specialized Outposted Offices on global programmes directed at Headquarters in areas of their interest and competence;

ii) Regional and Outposted Offices

UNEP Regional Offices and Outposted Offices come across NGOs/Major Groups with special needs and competencies. These Regional and Outposted Offices shall:

a) maintain their own direct links with NGOs/Major Groups operating in their region, including groups working at the national and community level, to map out areas for collaboration with UNEP and initiate and/or undertake joint initiatives;

b) encourage regional and international networks based in their regions to participate in decision-making fora like Governing Council and facilitate their attendance, subject to the availability of resources;

c) ensure two-way information flow with NGOs/Major Groups and continually assess their needs in this regard;

d) report to HQ on-going and planned collaboration with NGOs/Major Groups so that this is accurately reflected in overviews of collaboration with the non-governmental sector(s) and is available for emulation by other regions, offices and programme units;

e) develop and maintain NGO/Major Groups databases relevant to their region and participate in the design and updating of global ones kept by HQ for purposes of effective records-keeping and efficient back-up to partners.

5. Terms of Agreement

Agreements with individual NGOs/Major Groups organizations shall be the responsibility of relevant Programme Unit, Regional or Outposted Office and shall be based on project formats and procedures given by the Project Design and Evaluation Unit; Agreements entered into by all units and offices with NGOs/Major Groups shall be notified to the Headquarters for Major Groups reporting;

6. Funding

The financing of collaboration with NGOS/Major Groups and other partners in the non-governmental sector(s) has to be budgeted for in the estimates of individual programme units and offices. The Division of Policy Development and Law, shall within available resources budget and solicit funds for outreach activities, including funds for use by Regional Offices. Trust fund instruments shall also be developed for various sectors as needed in order to attract earmarked funds from donors to supplement allocations from the Environment Fund. In the climate of shrinking resources, UNEP as a whole shall whenever possible co-fundraise with NGO and other partners for mutually-agreed projects and programmes. Such fund-raising shall be governed by individual agreements or terms of sponsorship.

APPENDIX—2

CHARITABLE & RELIGIOUS TRUSTS ACT, 1920

[14 of 1920]

An Act to provide more effectual control over the administration of Charitable and Religious Trusts

Whereas it is expedient to provide facilities for the obtaining of information regarding trust created for public purposes of a charitable or religious nature, and to enable the trustees of such trusts to obtain the directions of a Court on certain matters, and to make special provision for the payment of the expenditure incurred in certain suits against the trustees of such trusts;

It is hereby enacted as follows: -

1. Short title and extent

(1) This Act may be called the Charitable and Religious Trusts Acts, 1920.

(2) It extends to the whole of India except the State of Jammu and Kashmir:

Provided that the Government at any State may, be notification in the Official Gazette, direct that this Act, or any specified part thereof, shall not extend to that State or any specified area therein, or to any specified trust or class of trusts.

2. Interpretation

In this Act, unless there is anything repugnant in the subject or context, "the Court" means the Court of the District Judge or any other Court empowered in that behalf by the State Government and includes the High Court in the exercise of its ordinary original civil jurisdiction.

3. Power to apply to the Court in respect of trusts of a charitable or religious nature

Save as hereinafter provided in this Act, any person having an interest in any express or constructive trust created or existing for a public purpose of a charitable or religious nature may apply by petition to the Court within the local limits of whose jurisdiction any substantial part of the subject-matter of the trust is situate to obtain an order embodying all or any of the following directions, namely:-

(1) directing the trustee to furnish the petitioner through the Court with particulars as to the nature and objects of the trust, and of the value condition, management and application of the subject-matter of the trust, and of the income belonging thereto, or as any of these matters, and

(2) directing that the accounts of the trusts shall be examined and audited:

Provided that no person shall apply for any such direction in respect of accounts relating to a period more than three years prior to the date of the petition.

4. Contents and verification of petition

(1) The petition shall show in what way the petitioner claims to be interested in the trust, and shall specify, as far as may be, the particulars and the audit which he seeks to obtain.

(2) The petition shall be in writing and shall be signed and verified in the manner prescribed by the Code of Civil Procedure, 1908 (5 of 1908), for signing and verifying plaints.

5. Procedure on petition

(1) If the court on receipt of a petition under section 3, after taking such evidence and making such inquiry, if any, as it may consider necessary, is of opinion that the trust to which the petition relates is a trust to which this Act applies, and that the petitioner has an interest therein, it shall fix a date for the hearing of the petition, and shall cause a copy thereof, together with notice of the date so fixed, to be served on the trustee and upon any other person to whom in its opinion notice of the petition should be given.

(2) On the date fixed for the hearing of the petition, or on any subsequent date to which the hearing may be adjourned, the Court shall proceed to hear the petitioner and the trustee, if he appears, and any other person who has appeared in consequence of the notice, or who it considers ought to be heard, and shall make such further inquiries, if any, as it thinks fit. The trustee may and, if so required by the court, shall at the time of the first hearing or within such time as the Court may permit present a written statement of his case. If he does present a written statement, the statement shall be signed and verified in the manner prescribed by the Code of Civil Procedure, 1908 (5 of 1908), for signing and verifying pleadings.

(3) If any person appears at the hearing of the petition and either denies the existence of the trust or denies that it is a trust to which this Act applies, and undertakes to institute within three months a suit for a declaration to that effect and for any other appropriate relief, the court shall order a stay of

the proceedings and, if such suit is so instituted, shall continue the stay until the suit is finally decided.

(4) If no such undertaking is given, or if after the expiry of the three months no such suit has been instituted, the Court shall itself decide the question.

(5) On completion of the inquiry provided for in sub-section (2), the Court shall either dismiss the petition or pass thereon such other order as it thinks fit:

Provided that, where a suit has been instituted in accordance with the provisions of sub-section (3), no order shall be passed by the Court which conflicts with the final decision therein.

(6) Save as provided in this section, the Court shall not try or determine any question of title between the petitioner and any person claiming title adversely to the trust.

6. Failure of trustee to comply with order under Section 5

If a trustee without reasonable excuse fails to comply with an order made under sub-section (5) of section 5, such trustee shall, without prejudice to any other penalty or liability which he may incur under any law for the time being in force, be deemed to have committed a breach of trust affording ground for a suit under the provisions of section 92 of the Code of Civil Procedure, 1908 (5 of 1908), and any such suit may, so far as it is based on such failure, be instituted without the previous consent of the Advocate General.

7. Powers of trustee to apply for directions

(1) Save as hereinafter provided in this Act, any trustee

of an express or constructive trust created or existing for public purpose of a charitable or religious nature may apply by petition to the Court, within the local limits of whose jurisdiction any substantial part of the subject-matter of the trust is situate, for the opinion, advise or direction of the Court on any question affecting the management or administration of the trust property, and the Court shall give its opinion, advice or direction, as the case may be, thereon:

Provided that the Court shall not be bound to give such opinion, advice or direction on any question which it considers to be a question not proper for summary disposal.

(2) The Court on a petition under sub-section (1), may either give its opinion, advice or direction thereon forthwith, or fix a date for the hearing of the petition, and may direct a copy thereof, together with notice of the date so fixed, to be served on such of the persons interested in the trust, or to be published for information in such manner, as it thinks fit.

(3) On any date fixed under sub-section (2) or any subsequent date to which the hearing may be adjourned, the Court, before giving any opinion, advice or direction, shall afford a reasonable opportunity of being heard to all persons appearing in connection with the petition.

(4) A trustee stating in good faith the facts of any matter relating to the trust in a petition under sub-section (1), and acting upon the opinion, advice or direction of the Court given thereon, shall be deemed, as far as his own responsibility is concerned, to have discharged his duty as such trustee in the matter in respect of which the petition was made.

8. Costs of petition under this Act

The costs, charges and expenses of and incidental to any petition, and all proceedings in connection therewith, under the foregoing provisions of this Act, shall be in the discretion of the Court, which may direct the whole or any part of any such costs, charges and expenses to be met from the property or income of the trust in respect of which the petition is made, or to be borne and paid in such manner and by such persons as it thinks fit:

Provided that no such order shall be made against any person (other than the petitioner) who has not received notification of the petition and had a reasonable opportunity of being heard thereon.

9. Saving

No petition under the foregoing provisions of this Act in relation to any trust shall be entertained in any of the following circumstances, namely:-

(a) if a suit instituted in accordance with the provisions of section 92 of the Code of Civil Procedure, 1908 (5 of 1908), is pending in respect of the trust in question;

(b) If the trust property is vested in the Treasurer of Charitable Endowments, the Administrator-General, the Official Trustee, or any Society registered under the Societies Registration Act, 1860 (21 of 1860); or

(c) if a scheme for the administration of the trust property has been settled or approved by any Court of competent jurisdiction, or by any other authority acting under the provisions of any enactment.

10. Power of Courts as to costs in certain suits against trustees of charitable and religious trusts

(1) In any suit instituted under section 14 of the Religious Endowments Act, 1863, (20 of 1863) or under section 92 of the Code of Civil Procedure, 1908 (5 of 1908), the Court trying such suit may, if, on application of the plaintiff and after hearing the defendant and making such inquiry as it thinks fit, it is satisfied that such an order is necessary in the public interest, direct the defendant either to furnish security for any expenditure incurred or likely to be incurred by the plaintiff in instituting and maintaining such suit, or to deposit from any money in his hands as trustee of the trust to which the suit relates such sum as such Court considers sufficient to meet such expenditure in whole or in part.

(2) When any money has been deposited in accordance with an order made under sub-section (1), the Court may make over to the plaintiff the whole or any part of such sum for the conduct of the suit. Before making over any sum to the plaintiff, the Court shall take security from the plaintiff for the refund of the same in the event of such refund being subsequently ordered by the Court.

11. Provisions of the Code of Civil Procedure

(1) The provisions of the Code of Civil Procedure, 1908 (5 of 1908), relating to-

- (a) the proof of facts by affidavit,
- (b) the enforcing of the attendance of any person and his examination oath,

(c) the enforcing. of the production of documents, and

(d) the issuing of commissions,

shall apply to all proceedings under this Act, and the provisions relating to the service of summonses shall apply to the service of notice thereunder.

(2) The provisions of the said Code relating to the execution of decrees shall, so far as they are applicable, apply to the execution of orders under this Act.

12. Barring of appeals

No appeal shall lie from any order passed or against any opinion, advice or direction given under this Act.

APPENDIX—3

INDIAN TRUSTS ACT, 1882

[Act No. 2 of Year 1882]

CHAPTER I : PRELIMINARY

1. Short title and commencement

This Act may be called the Indian Trusts Act, 1882; and it shall come into force on the first day of March, 1882.

Local extent, Saving: It extends to the whole of India except the State of Jammu and Kashmir and the Andaman and Nicobar Islands; but the Central Government may, from time to time, by notification in the Official Gazette, extend it to the Andaman and Nicobar Islands or to any part thereof. But nothing herein contained affects the rules of Mohamedan law as to waqf, or the mutual relations of the members of an undivided family as determined by any customary, or personal law, or applies to public or private religious or charitable endowments or to trusts to distribute prizes taken in war among the captors; and nothing in the Second Chapter of this Act applies to trusts created before the said day.

2. Repeal of enactments

The statutes and Acts mentioned in the Schedule hereto annexed shall, to the extent mentioned in the said Schedule, be repealed, in the territories to which this Act for the time being extends.

3. Interpretation clause- "trust"

A "trust" is an obligation annexed to the ownership of property, and arising out of a confidence reposed in and accepted by the owner, or declared and accepted by him, for the benefit of another, or of another and the owner:

> *"author of the trust": "trustee": "beneficiary": "trust property": "beneficial interest": "instrument of trust":*
>
> the person who reposes or declares the confidence is called the "author of the trust": the person who accepts the confidence is called the "trustee": the person for whose benefit the confidence is accepted is called the "beneficiary": the subject-matter of the trust is called "trust-property" or "trust-money": the "beneficial interest" or "interest" of the beneficiary is his right against the trustee as owner of the trust-property; and the instrument, if any, by which the trust is declared is called the "instrument of trust";
>
> *"breach of trust":* a breach of any duty imposed on a trustee, as such, by any law for the time being in force, is called a "breach of trust".
>
> *"registered":* and in this Act, unless there be something repugnant in the subject or context, "registered" means registered under the law for the registration of documents for the time being in force.
>
> *"notice":* a person is said to have "notice" of a fact either when he actually knows that fact or when, but for wilful abstention from inquiry or gross negligence, he would have known it, or when information of the fact is given to or obtained by his agent, under the circumstances mentioned in the Indian Contract Act, 1872 (9 of 1872), section 229.

Expressions used herein and defined in the Indian Contract Act, 1872 (expressions defined in Act 9 of 1872), shall be deemed to have the meanings respectively attributed to them by that Act.

CHAPTER II : OF THE CREATION OF TRUSTS

4. Lawful purpose

A trust may be created for any lawful purpose. The purpose of a trust is lawful unless it is (a) forbidden by law, or (b) is of such a nature that, if permitted, it would defeat the provisions of any law, or (c) is fraudulent, or (d) involves or implies injury to the person or property of another, or (e) the court regards it as immoral or opposed to public policy.

Every trust of which the purpose is unlawful is void. And where a trust is created for two purposes, of which one is lawful and the other unlawful, and the two purposes, cannot be separated, the whole trust is void.

Explanation: In this section, the expression "law" includes, where the trust property is immovable and situate in a foreign country, the law of such country.

Illustrations

(a) A conveys property to B in trust to apply the profits to the nurture of female foundlings to be trained up as prostitutes. The trust is void

(b) A bequeaths property to B in trust to employ it in carrying on a smuggling business, and out of the profits thereof to support A's children. The trust is void.

(c) A, while in insolvent circumstances, transfers property to B in trust for A during his life, and after his death for B. A is declared an insolvent. The trust for A is invalid as against his creditors.

5. Trust of immovable property

No trust in relation to immovable property is valid unless declared by a non-testamentary instrument in writing signed by the author of the trust or the trustee and registered or by the will of the author of the trust or of the trustee.

Trust, of movable property: No trust in relation to movable property is valid unless declared as aforesaid, or unless the ownership of the property is transferred to the trustee.

These rules do not apply where they would operate so as to effectuate a fraud.

6. Creation of trust

Subject to the provisions of section 5, a trust is created when the author of the trust indicates with reasonable certainty by any words or acts (a) an intention on his part to create thereby a trust, (b) the purpose of the trust, (c) the beneficiary, and (d) the trust-property, and (unless the trust is declared by will or the author of the trust is himself to be the trustee) transferred the trust-property to the trustee.

Illustrations

(a) A bequeaths certain property to B, "having the fullest confidence that he will dispose of it for the benefit of C". This creates a trust so far as regards A and C.

(b) A bequeaths certain property to B, "hoping he will continue it in the family". This does not create a trust, as the beneficiary is not indicated with reasonable certainty.

(c) A bequeaths certain property to B, requesting him to distribute it amongst such members of C's family as B should think most deserving. This does not create a trust, for the beneficiaries are not indicated with reasonable certainty.

(d) A bequeaths certain property to B, desiring him to divide the bulk of it among C's children. This does not create a trust, for the trust-property is not indicated with sufficient certainty.

(e) A bequeaths a ship and stock-in-trade to B, on condition that he pays A's debts and legacy to C. This is a condition, not a trust for A's creditors and C.

7. Who may create trusts

A trust may be created-

(a) by every person competent to contract, and

(b) with the permission of a principal civil court of original jurisdiction, by or on behalf of a minor,

but subject in each case to the law for the time being in force as to the circumstances and extent in and to which the author of the trust may dispose of the trust property.

8. Subject matter of trust

The subject-matter of a trust must be property transferable to the beneficiary. It must not be merely beneficial interest under a subsisting trust.

9. Who may be beneficiary

Every person capable of holding property may be a beneficiary.

Disclaimer by beneficiary : A proposed beneficiary may renounce his interest under the trust by disclaimer addressed to the trustee, or by setting up, with notice of the trust, a claim inconsistent therewith.

10. Who may be trustee

Every person capable of holding property may be a trustee; but, where the trust involves the exercise of discretion, he cannot execute it unless he is competent to contract.

No one bound *to accept trust :* No one is bound to accept a trust.

Acceptance of trust: A trust is accepted by any words or acts of the trustee indicating with reasonable certainty such acceptance.

Disclaimer of trust : Instead of accepting a trust, the intended trustee may, within a reasonable period, disclaim it, and such disclaimer shall prevent the trust-property from vesting in him.

A disclaimer by one of two or more co-trustees vests the trust-property in the other or others, and makes him or them sole trustee or trustees from the date of the creation of the trust.

Illustrations

(a) A bequeaths certain property to B and C, his executors, as trustees for D. B and C prove A's will. This is in itself an acceptance of the trust, and B and C hold the property in trust for D.

(b) A transfers certain property to B in trust to sell it and to pay out of the proceeds A's debts. B accepts the trust and sells the property. So far as regards B, a trust of the proceeds is created for A's creditors.

(c) A bequeaths a lakh of rupees to B upon certain trusts and appoints him his executor. B severs the lakh from the general assets and appropriates it to the specific purpose. This is an acceptance of the trust.

CHAPTER III : OF THE DUTIES AND LIABILITIES OF TRUSTEES

11. Trustee to execute trust

The trustee is bound to fulfil the purpose of the trust, and to obey the directions of the author of the trust given at the time of its creation, except as modified by the consent of all the beneficiaries being competent to contract.

Where the beneficiary is incompetent to contract, his consent may, for the purposes of this section, be given by a principal civil court of original jurisdiction.

Nothing in this section shall be deemed to require a trustee to obey any direction when to do so would be impracticable, illegal or manifestly injurious to the beneficiaries.

Explanation: Unless a contrary intention be expressed, the purpose of a trust for the payment of debts shall be deemed to be (a) to pay only the debts of the author of the trust existing and recoverable at the date of the instrument of trust, or, when such instrument is a will, at the date of his death, and (b) in the case of debts not bearing interest, to make such payment without interest.

Illustrations

(a) A, a trustee, is simply authorised to sell certain land by public auction. He cannot sell the land by private contract.

(b) A, a trustee of certain land for X, Y and Z, is authorized to sell the land to B for a specified sum. X, Y and Z, being competent to contract, consent that A may sell the land to C for a less sum. A may sell the land accordingly.

(c) A, a trustee for B and her children, is directed by the author of the trust to lend, on B's request, trust-property to B's husband C, on the security of his bond. C becomes insolvent and B requests A to make the loan. A may refuse to make it.

12. Trustee to inform himself of state of trust-property

A trustee is bound to acquaint himself, as soon as possible, with the nature and circumstances of the trust-property; to obtain, where necessary, a transfer of the trust property to himself; and (subject to the provisions of the instrument of trust) to get in trust-moneys invested on insufficient or hazardous security.

Illustrations

(a) The trust-property is a debt outstanding on personal security. The instrument of trust gives the trustee no discretionary power to leave the debt so outstanding. The trustee's duty is to recover the debt without unnecessary delay.

(b) The trust-property is money in the hands of one of two co-trustees. No discretionary power is given by the instrument of trust. The other co-trustee must not allow the former to retain the money for a longer period than the circumstances of the case required.

13. Trustee to protect title to trust-property

A trustee is bound to maintain and defend all such suits, and (subject to the provisions of the instrument of trust) to take such other steps as, regard being had to the nature and amount or value of the trust-property, may be reasonably requisite for the preservation of the trust-property and the assertion or protection of the title thereto.

Illustration

The trust-property is immovable property which has been given to the author of the trust by an unregistered instrument. Subject to the provisions of the Indian Registration Act, 1877 (3 of 1877), the trustee's duty is to cause the instrument to be registered.

14. Trustee not to set up title adverse to beneficiary

The trustee must not for himself or another set up or aid any title to the trust-property adverse to the interest of the beneficiary.

15. Care required from trustee

A trustee is bound to deal with the trust-property as carefully as a man of ordinary prudence would deal with such property if it were his own; and, in the absence of a contract to the contrary, a trustee so dealing is not responsible for the loss, destruction or deterioration of the trust-property.

Illustrations

(a) A, living in Calcutta, is a trustee for B, living in

Bombay. A remits trust funds to B by bills drawn by a person of undoubted credit in favour of the trustee as such, and payable at Bombay. The bills are dishonoured. A is not bound to make good the loss.

(b) A, trustee of leasehold property, directs the tenant to pay the rents on account of the trust to a banker, B, then in credit. The rents are accordingly paid to B, and A leaves the money with B only till wanted. Before the money is drawn out, B becomes insolvent. A, having had no reason to believe that B was in insolvent circumstances, is not bound to make good the loss.

(c) A, a trustee of two debts for B, releases one and compounds the other, in good faith, and reasonably believing that it is for B's interest to do so. A is not bound to make good any loss caused thereby to B.

(d) A, a trustee directed to sell the trust-property by auction, sells the same, but does not advertise the sale and otherwise fails in reasonable diligence in inviting competition. A is bound to make good the loss caused thereby to the beneficiary.

(e) A, a trustee for B, in execution of his trust, sells the trust-property, but from want of due diligence on his part fails to receive part of the purchase money. A is bound to make good the loss thereby caused to B.

(f) A, a trustee for B of a policy of insurance, has funds in hand for payment of the premiums. A neglects to pay the premiums, and the policy is consequently forfeited. A is bound to make good the loss to B.

(g) A bequeaths certain moneys to B and C as trustees, and authorizes them to continue trust-moneys upon the personal security of a certain firm in which A had himself invested them. A dies, and a change takes place in the firm. B and C must not permit the moneys to remain upon the personal security of the new firm.

(h) A, a trustee for B, allows the trust to be executed solely by his co-trustee C. C misapplies the trust-property. A is personally answerable for the loss resulting to B.

16. Conversion of perishable property

Where the trust is created for the benefit of several persons in succession, and the trust property is of a wasting nature or a future or reversionary interest, the trustee is bound, unless an intention to the contrary may be inferred from the instrument of trust, to convert the property into property of a permanent and immediately profitable character.

Illustrations

(a) A bequeaths to B all his property in trust for C during his life, and on his death for D, and on D's death for E. A's property consists of three leasehold houses, and there is nothing in A's will to show that he intended the houses to be enjoyed in specie. B should sell the houses, and invest the proceeds in accordance with section 20.

(b) A bequeaths to B his three leasehold houses in Calcutta and all the furniture therein in trust for C during his life, and on his death for D, and on D's death for E. Here an intention that the houses and furniture should be enjoyed in specie appears clearly, and B should not sell them.

17. Trustee to be impartial

Where there are more beneficiaries than one, the trustee is bound to be impartial, and must not execute the trust for the advantage of one at the expense of another.

Where the trustee has a discretionary power, nothing in this section shall be deemed to authorize the court to control the exercise reasonably and in good faith of such discretion.

Illustration

A, a trustee for B, C and D, is empowered to choose between several specified modes of investing the trust-property. A in good faith chooses one of these modes. The court will not interfere, although the result of the choice may be to vary the relative rights of B, C and D.

18. Trustee to prevent waste

Where the trust is created for the benefit of several persons in succession and one of them is in possession of the trust-property, if he commits, or threatens to commit, any act which is destructive or permanently injurious thereto, the trustee is bound to take measures to prevent such act.

19. Accounts and information

A trustee is bound (a) to keep clear and accurate accounts of the trust-property, and (b) at all reasonable times, at the request of the beneficiary, to furnish him with full and accurate information as to the amount and state of the trust-property.

20. Investment of trust-money

Where the trust-property consists of money and cannot be applied immediately or at an early date to the purposes of the trust, the trustee is bound (subject to any direction contained in the instrument of trust) to invest the money on the following securities, and on no others:

(a) in promissory notes, debentures, stock or other securities of any State Government or of the Central Government, or of the United Kingdom of Great Britain and Ireland:

Provided that securities, both the principal whereof and the interest whereon shall have been fully and unconditionally guaranteed by any such government, shall be deemed, for the purposes of this clause, to be securities of such government;

(b) in bonds, debentures and annuities charged or secured by the Parliament of the United Kingdom before the fifteenth day of August, 1947 on the revenues of India or of the Governor General in Council or of any province:

Provided that, after the fifteenth day of February, 1916, no money shall be invested in any such annuity being a terminable annuity unless a sinking fund has been established in connection with such annuity; but nothing in this proviso shall apply to investments made before the date aforesaid.

(bb) in India three and a half per cent stock, India three per cent stock, India two and a half per cent stock or any other capital stock which before the 15th day of August, 1947, was issued by the Secretary of State for India in Council under the authority of an Act of Parliament of the United kingdom and charged on the revenues of India or which was issued by the Secretary of State on behalf of the Governor-General in Council under the provisions of Part XIII of the Government of India Act, 1935;

(c) in stock or debentures of, or shares in, Railway or other companies the interest whereon shall have been guaranteed by the Secretary of State for India in Council or by the Central Government or in debentures of the Bombay Provincial Co-operative Bank Limited, the interest whereon shall have been guaranteed, by the Secretary of State for India in Council or the State Government of Bombay;

(d) in debentures or other securities for money issued, under the authority of any Central Act or Provincial Act or State Act, by or on behalf of any municipal body, port trust or city improvement trust in any Presidency-town, or in Rangoon town, or by or on behalf of the trustees of the port of Karachi:

Provided that after the 31st day of March, 1948, no money shall be invested in any securities issued by or on behalf of a municipal body, port trust or city improvement trust in Rangoon town, or by or on behalf of the trustees of the port of Karachi ;

(e) On a first mortgage of immovable property situate in any part of the territories to which this Act extends [1][* * *]:

Provided that the property is not a leasehold for a term of years and that the value of the property exceeds by one-third, or, if consisting of buildings, exceeds by one-half, the mortgage-money;

[2][(ee) in units issued by the Unit Trust of India under any unit scheme made under section 21 of the Unit Trust of India Act, 1963 (52 of 1963); or]

(f) on any other security expressly authorized by the instrument of trust, [2][or by the Central Government by the notification in the Official Gazette] or by any rule which the High Court may from time to time prescribe in this behalf:

Provided that, where there is a person competent to contract and entitled in possession to receive the income of the trust-property for his life, or for any greater estate, no investment on any security mentioned or referred to in clauses (d), (e) and (f) shall be made without his consent in writing.

20A. Power to purchase redeemable stock at a premium

(1) A trustee may invest in any of the securities mentioned or referred to in section 20, notwithstanding that the same may be redeemable and that the price exceeds the redemption value:

Provided that a trustee may not purchase at a price exceeding its redemption value any security mentioned or referred to in clauses (c) and (d) of section 20 which is liable to be redeemed within fifteen years of the date of purchase at par or at some other fixed rate, or purchase any such security as is mentioned or referred to in the said clauses which is liable to be redeemed at par or at some other fixed rate at a price exceeding fifteen per centum above par or such other fixed rate.

(2) A trustee may retain until redemption any redeemable stock, fund or security which may have been purchased in accordance with this section.

21. Mortgage of land Pledged to government under Act 26 of 1871-Deposit in government savings bank

Nothing in section 20 shall apply to investments made before this Act comes into force, or shall be deemed to Preclude an investment on a mortgage of immovable property already pledged as security for an advance under the Land Improvement Act, 1871 (26 of 1871), or in case the trust-money does not exceed three thousand rupees, a deposit thereof in a government savings bank.

22. Sale by trustee directed to sell within specified time

Where a trustee directed to sell within a specified time extends such time, the burden of proving, as between himself and the beneficiary, that the latter is not prejudiced by the extension lies upon the trustee, unless the extension has been authorised by a principal civil court of original jurisdiction.

Illustration

A bequeaths property to B, directing him with all convenient speed and within five years to sell it, and apply the proceeds for the benefit of C. In the exercise of reasonable discretion, B postpones the sale for six years. The sale is not thereby rendered invalid, but C, alleging that he has been injured by the postponement, institutes a suit against B to obtain compensation. In such suit the burden of proving that C has not been injured lies on B.

23. Liability for breach of trust

Where the trustee commits a breach of trust, he is liable to make good the loss which the trust-property or the beneficiary has thereby sustained, unless the beneficiary has by fraud induced the trustee to commit the breach, or the beneficiary, being competent to contract, has himself, without coercion or undue influence having been brought to bear on him, concurred in the breach, or subsequently acquiesced therein, with full knowledge of the facts of the case and of his rights as against the trustee.

A trustee committing a breach of trust is not liable to pay interest except in the following cases :-

(a) where he has actually received interest;

(b) where the breach consists in unreasonable delay in paying trust-money to the beneficiary;

(c) where the trustee ought to have received interest, but has not done so;

(d) where he may be fairly presumed to have received interest.

He is liable, in case (a), to account for the interest actually received, and, in case (b), (c) and (d), to account for simple interest at the rate of six per cent per annum, unless the court otherwise directs;

(e) where the breach consists in failure to invest trust-money and to accumulate the interest or dividends thereon, he is liable to account for compound interest (with half-yearly rests) at the same rate;

(f) where the breach consists in the employment of trust-property or the proceeds thereof in trade or business he is liable to account, at the option of the beneficiary, either for compound interest (with half-yearly rests) at the same rate, or for the net profits made by such employment.

Illustrations

(a) A trustee improperly leaves trust-property

outstanding, and it is consequently lost; he is liable to make good the property lost, but he is not liable to pay interest thereon.

(b) A bequeaths a house to B in trust to sell it and pay the proceeds to C. B neglects to sell the house for a great length of time, whereby the house is deteriorated and its market price falls. B is answerable to C for the loss.

(c) A trustee is guilty of unreasonable delay in investing trust money in accordance with section 20, or in paying it to the beneficiary. The trustee is liable to pay interest thereon for the period of the delay.

(d) The duty of the trustee is to invest trust-money in any of the securities mentioned in section 20, clauses (a), (b), (c) or (d). Instead of so doing, he retains the money in his hands. He is liable, at the option of the beneficiary, to be charged either with the amount of the principal money and interest, or with the amount of such securities as he might have purchased with the trust-money when the investment should have been made, and the intermediate dividends and interest thereon.

(e) The instrument of trust directs the trustee to invest trust-money either in any of such securities or on mortgage of immovable property. The trustee does neither. He is liable for the principal money and interest.

(f) The instrument of trust directs the trustee to invest trust-money in any of such securities and to accumulate the dividends thereon. The trustee disregards the direction. He is liable, at the option of the beneficiary, to be charged either with the amount of the principal money and compound interest, or with the amount of such securities as he might have purchased with the trust-money when the investment should have been made, together with the amount of the accumulation which would have arisen from a proper investment of the intermediate dividends.

(g) Trust-property is invested in one of the securities mentioned in section 20, clauses (a), (b), (c) or (d). The trustee sells such security for some purpose not authorized by the terms of the instrument of trust. He is liable, at the option of the beneficiary, either to replace the security with the intermediate dividends and interest thereon, or to account for the proceeds of the sale with interest thereon.

(h) The trust-property consists of land. The trustee sells the land to a purchaser for a consideration without notice of the trust. The trustee is liable, at the option of the beneficiary, to purchase other land of equal value to be settled upon the like trust, or to be charged with the proceeds of the said with interest.

24. No set-off allowed to trustee

A trustee who is liable for a loss occasioned by a breach of trust in respect of one portion of the trust-Property cannot set-off against his liability a gain which has accrued to another portion of the trust property through another and distinct breach of trust.

25. Non-liability for predecessor's default

Where a trustee succeeds another, he is not, as such, liable for the acts or defaults of his predecessor.

26. Non-liability for co-trustee's default

Subject to the provisions of sections 13 and 15, one trustee is not, as such, liable for a breach of trust committed by his co-trustee:

Provided that, in, the absence of an express declaration to the contrary in the instrument of trust, a trustee is so liable-

(a) where he has delivered trust-property to his co-trustee without seeing to its proper application;

(b) where he allows his co-trustee to receive trust-property and fails to make due enquiry as to the co-trustee's dealings therewith, or allows him to retain it longer than the circumstances of the case reasonably require;

(c) where he becomes aware of a breach of trust committed or intended by his co-trustee, and either actively conceals it or does not within a reasonable time take proper steps to protect the beneficiary's interest.

Joining in receipt for conformity

A co-trustee who joins in signing a receipt for trust-property and proves that he has not received the same is not answerable, by reason of such signature only, for loss or mis-application of the property by his co-trustee.

Illustration

A bequeaths certain property to B and C, and directs them to sell it and invest the proceeds for the benefit of D. B and C accordingly sell the property, and the purchase money is received by B and retained in his hands. C pays no attention to the matter for two years and then calls on

B to make the investment. B is unable to do so, becomes insolvent, and the purchase-money is lost. C may be compelled to make good the amount.

27. Several liability of co-trustees

Where co-trustees jointly commit a breach of trust, or where one of them by his neglect enables the other to commit a breach of trust, each is liable to the beneficiary for the whole of the loss occasioned by such breach.

Contribution as between co-trustees

But as between the trustees themselves, if one be less guilty than another and has had to refund the loss, the former may compel the latter, or his legal representative to the extent of the assets he has received, to make good such loss; and if all be equally guilty, any one or more of the trustees who has had to refund the loss may compel the others to contribute.

Nothing in this section shall be deemed to authorize a trustee who has been guilty of fraud to institute a suit to compel contribution.

28. Non-liability of trustee paying without notice of transfer by beneficiary

When any beneficiary's interest becomes vested in another person, and the trustee, not having notice of the vesting, pays or delivers trust-property to the person who would have been entitled thereto in the absence of such vesting, the trustee is not liable for the property so paid or delivered.

29. Liability of trustee where beneficiary's interest is forfeited to the government

When the beneficiary's interest is forfeited or awarded

by legal adjudication to the government, the trustee is bound to hold the trust-property to the extent of such interest for the benefit of such person in such manner as the State Government may direct in this behalf.

30. Indemnity of trustees

Subject to the provisions of the instrument of trust and of sections 23 and 26, trustees shall be respectively chargeable only for such moneys, stocks, funds and securities as they respectively actually receive, and shall not be answerable the one for the other of them, nor for any banker, broker or other person in whose hands any trust-property may be placed, nor for the insufficiency or deficiency of any stocks, funds or securities, nor otherwise for involuntary losses.

CHAPTER IV : OF THE RIGHTS AND POWERS OF TRUSTEES

31. Right to title deed

A trustee is entitled to have in his possession the instrument of trust and all the documents of title (if any) relating solely to the trust-property.

32. Right to reimbursement of expenses

Every trustee may reimburse himself, or pay or discharge out of the trust-property, all expenses properly incurred in or about the execution of the trust, or the realization, preservation or benefit of the trust-property, or the protection or support of the beneficiary.

If he pays such expenses out of his own pocket he has a first charge upon the trust-property for such expenses and interest thereon; but such charge (unless the expenses have been incurred with the sanction of a principal civil court of original jurisdiction) shall be enforced only by prohibiting any disposition of the trust-property without previous payment of such expenses and interest.

If the trust property fail, the trustee is entitled to recover from the beneficiary personally on whose behalf he acted, and at whose request, expressed or implied, he made the payment, the amount of such expenses.

Right to be recouped for erroneous over-payment

Where a trustee has by mistake made an over-payment to the beneficiary, he may reimburse the trust-property out of the beneficiary's interest. If such interest fail, the trustee is entitled to recover from the beneficiary personally the amount of such over-payment.

33. Right to indemnity from gainer by breach of trust

A person other than a trustee who has gained an advantage from a breach of trust must indemnify the trustee to the extent of the amount actually received by such person under the breach; and where he is a beneficiary the trustee has a charge on his interest for such amount.

Nothing in this section shall be deemed to entitle a trustee to be indemnified who has, in committing the breach of trust, been guilty of fraud.

34. Right to apply to court for opinion in management of trust-property

Any trustee may, without instituting a suit, apply by petition to a principal civil court of original jurisdiction for its opinion, advice or direction on any present questions respecting the management or administration of the trust-property other than questions of detail, difficulty or importance, not proper in the opinion of the court for summary disposal.

A copy of such petition shall be served upon, and the hearing thereof may be attended by, such of the persons interested in the application as the court thinks fit.

The trustee stating in good faith the facts in such petition, and acting upon the opinion, advice or direction given by the court shall be deemed, so far as regards his own responsibility, to have discharged his duty as such trustee in the subject-matter of the application.

The costs of every application under this section shall be in the discretion of the court to which it is made.

35. Right to settlement of accounts

When the duties of a trustee, as such, are completed, he is entitled to have the accounts of his administration of the trust-property examined and settled; and, where nothing is due to the beneficiary under the trust, to an acknowledgement in writing to that effect.

36. General authority of trustee

In addition to the powers expressly conferred by this Act and by the instrument of trust, and subject to the restriction, if any, contained in such instrument, and to the provisions of section 17, a trustee may do all acts which are reasonable and proper for the realization, protection or benefit of the trust-property, and for the protection or support of a beneficiary who is not competent to contract.

Except with the permission of a principal civil court of original jurisdiction, no trustee shall lease trust-property for a term exceeding twenty-one years from the date of executing the lease, nor without reserving the best yearly rent than can be reasonably obtained.

37. Power to sell in lots and either by public auction or private contract

Where the trustee is empowered to sell any trust-property, he may sell the same subject to prior charges or not, and either together or in lots, by public auction or private contract, and either at one time or at several times, unless the instrument of trust otherwise directs.

38. Power to sell under special conditions-Power to buy-in and re-sell

The trustee making any such sale may insert such reasonable stipulations either as to title or evidence of title, or otherwise, in any conditions of sale or contract for sale, as he thinks fit; and may also buy-in the property or any part thereof at any sale by auction, and rescind or vary any contract for sale, and re-sell the property so bought in, or as to which the contract is so rescinded, without being responsible to the beneficiary for any loss occasioned thereby.

Time Allowed selling trust-property

Where a trustee is directed to sell trust-property or to invest trust-money in the purchase of property, he may exercise a reasonable discretion as to the time of effecting the sale or purchase.

Illustrations

(a) A bequeaths property to B, directing him to sell it with all convenient speed and pay the proceeds to C. This does not render an immediate sale imperative.

(b) A bequeaths property to B, directing him to sell it at such time and in such manner as he shall think fit and invest the proceeds for the benefit of C. This does not authorize B, as between him and C, to postpone the sale to an indefinite period.

39. Power to convey

For the purpose of completing any such sale, the trustee shall have power to convey or otherwise dispose of the property sold in such manner as may be necessary.

40. Power to vary investments

A trustee may, at his discretion, call in any trust-property invested in any security and invest the same on any of the securities mentioned or referred to in section 20, and from time to time vary any such investments for others of the same nature:

Provided that, where there is a person competent to contract and entitled at the time to receive the income of the trust property for his life, or for any greater estate, no such change of investment shall be made without his consent in writing.

41. Power to apply property of minors, etc. for their maintenance, etc.

Where any property is held by a trustee in trust for a minor, such trustee may, at his discretion, pay to the guardians (if any) of such minor, or otherwise apply for or towards his maintenance or education or advancement in life, or the reasonable expenses of his religious worship, marriage or funeral, the whole or any part of the income to which he may be entitled in respect of such property; and such trustee shall accumulate all the residue of such income by way of compound interest, by investing the same and the resulting income thereof from time to time in any of the securities mentioned or referred to in section 20, for the benefit of the person who shall ultimately become entitled to the property from which such accumulations have arisen:

Provided that such trustee may, at any time, if he thinks fit, apply the whole or any part of such accumulations as if the same were part of the income arising in the then current year.

Where the income of the trust-property is insufficient for the minor's maintenance or education or advancement in life, or the reasonable expenses of his religious worship, marriage or funeral, the trustee may, with the permission of a principal civil court of original jurisdiction, but not otherwise, apply the whole or any part of such property for or towards such maintenance, education, advancement or expenses.

Nothing in this section shall be deemed to affect the provisions of any local law for the time being in force relating to the persons and property of minors.

42. Power to give receipts

Any trustees or trustee may give a receipt in writing for any money, securities or other movable property payable, transferable or deliverable to them or him by reason, or in thc exercise of any trust or power; and, in the absence of fraud, such receipt shall discharge the person paying, transferring or delivering the same therefrom, and from seeing to the application thereof, or being accountable for any loss or misapplication thereof.

43. Power to compound, etc.

Two or more trustees acting together may; if and as they think fit,-

(a) accept any composition or any security for any debt or for any property claimed;

(b) allow any time for payment of any debt;

(c) compromise, compound, abandon, submit to arbitration or otherwise settle any debt, account, claim or thing whatever relating to the trust; and

(d) for any of those purposes, enter into, give, execute and do such agreements, instruments of composition or arrangement, releases and other things as to them seem expedient, without being responsible for any loss occasioned by any act or thing so done by them in good faith.

The powers conferred by this section on two or more trustees acting together may be exercised by a sole acting trustee when by the instrument of trust, if any, a sole trustee is authorized to execute the trusts and powers thereof.

This section applies only if and as far as a contrary intention is not expressed in the instrument of trust, if any, and shall have effect subject to the terms of that instrument and to the provisions therein contained.

This section applies only to trusts created after this Act comes into force.

44. Power to several trustees of whom one disclaims or dies

When an authority to deal with the trust-property is given to several trustees and one of them disclaims or dies, the authority may be exercised by the continuing trustees, unless from the terms of the instrument of trust it is apparent that the authority is to be exercised by a number in excess of the number of the remaining trustees.

45. Suspension of trustee's powers by decree

Where a decree has been made in a suit for the execution of a trust, the trustee must not exercise any of his powers except in conformity with such decree, or with the sanction of the court by which the decree has been made, or, where an appeal against the decree is pending, of the appellate court.

CHAPTER V: OF THE DISABILITIES OF TRUSTEES

46. Trustee cannot renounce after acceptance

A trustee who has accepted the trust cannot afterwards renounce it except (a) with the permission of a principal civil court of original jurisdiction, or (b) if the beneficiary is competent to contract, with his consent, or (c) by virtue of a special power in the instrument of trust.

47. Trustee cannot delegate

A trustee cannot delegate his office or any of his duties either to a co-trustee or to a stranger, unless (a) the instrument of trust so provides, or (b) the delegation is in the regular course of business, or (c) the delegation is necessary, or (d) the beneficiary, being competent to contract, consents to the delegation.

Explanation: The appointment of an attorney or proxy to do an act merely ministerial and involving no independent discretion is not a delegation within the meaning of this section.

Illustrations

(a) A bequeaths certain property to B and C on certain trusts to be executed by them or the survivor of them or the assigns of such survivor. B dies. C may bequeath the trust-property to D and E upon the trusts of A's will.

(b) A is a trustee of certain property with power to sell the same. A may employ an auctioneer to effect the sale.

(c) A bequeaths to B fifty houses let at monthly rents in trust to collect the rents and pay them to C. B may employ a proper person to collect these rents.

48. Co-trustees cannot act singly

When there are more trustees than one, all must join in the execution of the trust, except where the instrument of trust otherwise provides.

49. Control of discretionary power

Where a discretionary power conferred on a trustee is not exercised reasonably and in good faith, such power may be controlled by a principal civil court of original jurisdiction.

50. Trustee may not charge for services

In the absence of express directions to the contrary contained in the instrument of trust or of a contract to the contrary entered into with the beneficiary or the court at the time of accepting the trust, a trustee has no right to remuneration for his trouble, skill and loss of time in executing the trust.

Nothing in this section applies to any Official Trustee,

Administrator General, Public Curator, or person holding a certificate of administration.

51. Trustee may not use trust property for his own profit

A trustee may not use or deal with the trust-property for his own profit or for any other purpose unconnected with the trust.

52. Trustee for sale or his agent may not buy

No trustee whose duty it is to sell trust-property, and no agent employed by such trustee for the purpose of the sale, may, directly or indirectly, buy the same or any interest therein, on his own account or as agent for a third person.

53. Trustee may not buy beneficiary's interest without permission

Not trustee, and no person who has recently ceased to be a trustee, may, without the permission of a principal civil court of original jurisdiction, buy or become mortgagee or lessee of the trust-property or any part thereof; and such permission shall not be given unless the proposed purchase, mortgage or lease is manifestly for the advantage of the beneficiary.

Trustee for purchase

And no trustee whose duty it is to buy or to obtain a mortgage or lease of particular property for the beneficiary may buy it, or any part thereof, or obtain a mortgage or lease of it, or any part thereof, for himself.

54. Co-trustees may not lend to one of themselves

A trustee or co-trustee whose duty it is to invest trust-money on mortgage or personal security must not invest it on a mortgage by, or on the personal security of, himself or one of his co-trustees.

CHAPTER VI : OF THE RIGHTS AND LIABILITIES OF THE BENEFICIARY

55. Rights to rents and profits

The beneficiary has, subject to the provisions of the instrument of trust, a right to the rents and profits of the trust property.

56. Right to specific execution

The beneficiary is entitled to have the intention of the author of the trust specifically executed to the extent of the beneficiary's interest;

Right to transfer of possession

and, where there is only one beneficiary and he is competent to contract, or where there are several beneficiaries and they are competent to contract and all of one mind, he or they may require the trustee to transfer the trust-property to him or them, or to such person as he or they may direct.

When property has been transferred or bequeathed for the benefit of a married woman, so that she shall not have power to deprive herself of her beneficial interest, nothing in the second clause of this section applies to such property during her marriage.

Illustrations

(a) Certain government securities are given to trustees upon trust to accumulate the interest until A attains the age of 24, and then to transfer the gross amount to him. A on attaining majority may, as the person exclusively interested in the trust-property, require the trustees to transfer it immediately to him.

(b) A bequeaths Rs. 10,000 to trustees upon trust to purchase an annuity for B, who has attained his majority and is otherwise competent to contract, B may claim the Rs. 10,000.

(c) A transfers certain property to B and directs him to sell or invest it for the benefit of C, who is competent to contract. C may elect to take the property in its original character.

57. Right to inspect and take copies of instrument of trust, accounts, etc.

The beneficiary has a right, as against the trustee and all persons claiming under him with notice of the trust, to inspect and take copies of the instrument of trust, the documents of title relating solely to the trust-property, the accounts of the trust-property and the vouchers (if any) by which they are supported, and the cases submitted and opinions taken by the trustee for his guidance in the discharge of his duty.

58. Right to transfer beneficial interest

The beneficiary, if competent to contract, may transfer his interest, but subject to the law for the time being in force as to the circumstances and extent in and to which he may dispose of such interest:

Provided that when property is transferred or bequeathed for the benefit of a married woman, so that she shall not have power to deprive herself of her beneficial interest, nothing in this section shall authorize her to transfer such interest during her marriage.

59. Right to sue for execution of trust

Where no trustees are appointed or all the trustees die, disclaim, or are discharged, or where for any other reason, the execution of a trust by the trustee is or becomes impracticable, the beneficiary may institute a suit for the execution of the trust, and the trust shall, so far as may be possible, be executed by the court until the appointment of a trustee or new trustee.

60. Right to proper trustees

The beneficiary has a right (subject to the provisions of the instrument of trust) that the trust-property shall be properly protected and held and administered by proper persons and by a proper number of such persons.

Explanation I: The following are not proper persons within the meaning of this section:

A person domiciled abroad: an alien enemy: a person having an interest inconsistent with that of the beneficiary: a person in insolvent circumstances; and, unless the personal law of the beneficiary allows otherwise, a married woman and a minor.

Explanation II: When the administration of the trust involves the receipt and custody of money, the number of trustees should be two at least.

Illustrations

(a) A, one of several beneficiaries, proves that B, the trustee, has improperly disposed of part of trust-property, or that the property is in danger from B's being in insolvent circumstances, or that he is incapacitated from acting as trustee. A may obtain a receiver of the trust-property.

(b) A bequeaths certain jewels to B in trust for C. B dies during A's lifetime; then A dies; C is entitled to have the property conveyed to a trustee for him.

(c) A conveys certain property to four trustees in trust for B. Three of the trustees die. B may institute a suit to have three new trustees appointed in the place of the deceased trustees.

(d) A conveys certain property to three trustees in trust for B. All the trustees disclaim. B may institute a suit to have three trustees appointed in place of the trustees so disclaiming.

(e) A, a trustee for B, refuses to act, or goes to reside permanently out of India or is declared an insolvent, or compounds with his creditors, or suffers a co-trustee to commit a breach of trust. B may institute a suit to have A removed and a new trustee appointed in his room.

61. Right to compel to any act of duty

The beneficiary has a right that his trustee shall be compelled to perform any particular act of his duty as such, and restrained from committing any contemplated or probable breach of trust.

Illustrations

(a) A contracts with B to pay him monthly Rs. 100 for the benefit of C. B writes and signs a letter declaring that he will hold in trust for C the money so to be paid. A fails to pay the money in accordance with his contract. C may compel B on a proper indemnity to allow C to sue on the contract in B's name.

(b) A is trustee of certain land, with a power to sell the same and pay the proceeds to B and C equally. A is about to make an improvident sale of the land. B may sue on behalf of himself and C for an injunction to restrain A from making the sale.

62. Wrongful purchase by trustee

Where a trustee has wrongfully bought trust-property, the beneficiary has a right to have the property declared subject to the trust or retransferred by the trustee, if it remains in his hands unsold, or, if it has been bought from him by any person with notice of the trust, by such person. But in such case the beneficiary must repay the purchase-money paid by the trustee, with interest, and such other expenses (if any) as he has properly incurred in the preservation of the property; and the trustee or purchaser must (a) account for the net profits of the property, (b) be charged with an occupation-rent, if he has been in actual possession of the property, and (c) allow the beneficiary to deduct a proportionate part of the purchase-money if the property has been deteriorated by the acts or omissions of the trustee or purchaser.

Nothing in this sections-

(a) impairs the rights of lessees and others, who, before the institution of a suit to have the property declared subject to the trust or retransferred, have contracted in good faith with the trustee or purchaser; or

(b) entitles the beneficiary to have the property declared subject to the trust or retransferred where he, being competent to contract, has himself, without coercion or undue influence having been brought to bear on him, ratified the sale to the trustee with full knowledge of the facts of the case and of his rights as against the trustee.

63. Following trust property-into the hands of third persons; into that into which it has been converted

Where trust-property comes into the hands of a third person inconsistently with the trust, the beneficiary may require him to admit formally, or may institute a suit for a declaration, that the property is comprised in the trust.

Where the trustee has disposed of trust-property and the money or other property which he has received therefor can be traced in his hands, or the hands of his legal representative or legatee, the beneficiary has, in respect thereof, rights as nearly as may be the same as his rights in respect of the original trust-property.

Illustrations

(a) A, a trustee for B of Rs. 10,000, wrongfully invests the Rs. 10,000 in the purchase of certain land. B is entitled to the land.

(b) A, a trustee, wrongfully purchased land in his own name, partly with his own money, partly with money subject to a trust for B. B is entitled to a charge on the land for the amount of the trust-money so misemployed.

64. Saving of rights of certain transferees

Nothing in section 63 entitles the beneficiary to any right in respect of property in thc hands of-

(a) a transferee in good faith for consideration without having notice of the trust, either when the purchase-money was paid, or when the conveyance was executed, or

(b) a transferee for consideration from such a transferee.

A judgement-creditor of the trustee attaching and purchasing trust-property is not a transferee for consideration within the meaning of this section.

Nothing in section 63 applies to money, currency notes and negotiable instruments in the hands of a bona fide holder to whom they have passed in circulation, or shall be deemed to affect the Indian Contract Act, 1872 (9 of 1872), section 108, or the liability of a person to whom a debt or charge is transferred.

65. Acquisition by trustee of trust-property wrongfully converted

Where a trustee wrongfully sells or otherwise transfers trust-property and afterwards himself becomes the owner of the property, the property again becomes subject to the trust, notwithstanding any want of notice on the part of intervening transferees in good faith for consideration.

66. Right in case of blended property

Where the trustee wrongfully mingles the trust-property with his own, the beneficiary is entitled to a charge on the whole fund for the amount due to him.

67. Wrongful employment by partner-trustee of trust-property for partnership purposes

If a partner, being a trustee, wrongfully employs trust-property in the business or on the account of the partnership, no other partner is liable therefor in his personal capacity to the beneficiaries, unless he had notice of the breach of trust.

The partners having such notice are jointly and severally liable for the breach of trust.

Illustrations

(a) A and B are partners. A dies, having bequeathed all his property to B in trust for Z, and appointed B his sole executor. B, instead of winding up the affairs of the partnership, retains all the assets in the business. Z may compel him, as partner, to account for so much of the profits as are derived from A's share of the capital. B is also answerable to Z for the improper employment of A's assets.

(b) A, a trader, bequeaths his property to B in trust for C. Appoints B his sole executor, and dies. B enters into partnership with X and Y in the same trade, and employs A's assets in the partnership business. B gives an indemnity to X and Y against the claims of C. Here X and Y are jointly liable with B to C as having knowingly become parties to the breach of trust committed by B.

68. Liability of beneficiary joining in breach of trust

Where one of several beneficiaries-

(a) joins in committing breach of trust, or

(b) knowingly obtains any advantage therefrom, without the consent of the other beneficiaries, or

(c) becomes aware of a breach of trust committed or intended to be committed, and either actually conceals it, or does not within a reasonable time take proper steps to protect the interests of the other beneficiaries, or

(d) has deceived the trustee and thereby induced him to commit a breach of trust, the other beneficiaries are entitled to have all his beneficial interest impounded as against him and all who claim under him (otherwise than as transferees for consideration without notice of the breach) until the loss caused by the breach has been compensated.

When property has been transferred or bequeathed for the benefit of a married woman, so that she shall not have power to deprive herself of her beneficial interest, nothing in this section applies to such property during her marriage.

69. Rights and liabilities of beneficiary's transferee

Every person to whom a beneficiary transfers his interest has the rights, and is subject to the liabilities, of the beneficiary in respect of such interest at the date of the transfer.

CHAPTER VII : OF VACATING THE OFFICE OF TRUSTEE

70. Office how vacated

The office of a trustee is vacated by his death or by his discharge from his office.

71. Discharge of trustee

The trustee may be discharged from his office only as follows:-

(a) by the extinction of the trust;

(b) by the completion of his duties under the trust;

(c) by such means as may be prescribed by the instrument of trust;

(d) by appointment under this Act of a new trustee in his place;

(e) by consent of himself and the beneficiary, or, where there are more beneficiaries than one, all the beneficiaries being competent to contract; or

(f) by the court to which a petition for his discharge is presented under this Act.

72. Petition to be discharged from trust

Notwithstanding the provisions of section 11, every trustee may apply by petition to a principal civil court of original jurisdiction to be discharged from his office; and if the court finds that there is sufficient reason for such discharge, it may discharge him accordingly, and direct his costs to be paid out of the trust-property. But where there is no such reason, the court shall not discharge him, unless a proper person can be found to take his place.

73. Appointment of new trustees on death, etc.

Whenever any person appointed a trustee disclaims, or any trustee, either original or substituted, dies, or is for a continuous period of six months absent from [3][India], or leaves [3][India] for the purpose of residing abroad, or is declared an insolvent, or desires to be discharged from the trust, or refuses or becomes, in the opinion of a principal civil court of original jurisdiction, unfit or personally incapable to act in the trust, or accepts an inconsistent trust, a new trustee may be appointed in his place by-

(a) the person nominated for that purpose by the instrument of trust (if any), or

(b) if there be no such person, or no such person able and willing to act, the author of the trust if he be alive and competent to contract, or the surviving or continuing trustees or trustee for the time being, or legal representative of the last surviving and continuing trustee, or (with the consent of the court) the retiring trustees, if they all retire simultaneously, or (with the like consent) the last retiring trustee.

Every such appointment shall be by writing under the hands of the person making it. On an appointment of a new trustee the number of trustees may be increased.

The Official Trustee may, with his consent and by the order of the court, be appointed under this section, in any case in which only one trustee is to be appointed and such trustee is to be the sole trustee.

The provisions of this section relative to a trustee who is dead include the case of a person nominated trustee in a will but dying before the testator, and those relative to a continuing trustee include a refusing or retiring trustee if willing to act in the execution of the power.

74. Appointment by court

Whenever any such vacancy or disqualification occurs and it is found impracticable to appoint a new trustee under section 73, the beneficiary may, without instituting a suit, apply by petition to a principal civil court of original jurisdiction for the appointment of a trustee or a new trustee, and the court may appoint a trustee or a new trustee accordingly.

Rule for selecting new *trustees* : In appointing new trustees, the court shall have regard (a) to the wishes of the author of the trust as expressed in or to be inferred from the instrument of trust; (b) to the wishes of the person, if any, empowered to appoint new trustees; (c) to the question whether the appointment will promote or impede the execution of the trust; and (d) where there are more beneficiaries than one, to the interests of all such beneficiaries.

75. Vesting of trust-property in new trustees

Whenever any new trustee is appointed under section 73 or section 74, all the trust-property for the time being vested in the surviving or continuing trustees or trustee, or in the legal representative of any trustee, shall become vested in such new trustee, either solely or jointly with the surviving or continuing trustees or trustee, as the case may require.

Powers of new trustees: Every new trustee so appointed, and every trustee appointed by a court either before or after the passing of this Act, shall have the same powers, authorities and discretions, and shall in all respects act, as if he had been originally nominated a trustee by the author of the trust.

76. Survival of trust

On the death or discharge of one of several co-trustees, the trust survives and the trust-property passes to the others, unless the instrument of trust expressly declares otherwise.

CHAPTER VIII: OF THE EXTINCTION OF TRUSTS

77. Trust how extinguished

A trust is extinguished-

(a) when its purpose is completely fulfilled; or

(b) when its purpose becomes unlawful; or

(c) when the fulfilment of its purpose becomes impossible by destruction of the trust-property or otherwise; or

(d) when the trust, being revocable, is expressly revoked.

78. Revocation of trust

A trust created by will may be revoked at the pleasure of the testator.

A trust otherwise created can be revoked only-

(a) where all the beneficiaries are competent to contract-by their consent;

(b) where the trust has been declared by a non-testamentary instrument or by word of mouth-in exercise of a power of revocation expressly reserved to the author of the trust; or

(c) where the trust is for the payment of the debts of the author of the trust, and has not been communicated to the creditors at the pleasure of the author of the trust.

Illustration

A conveys property to B in trust to sell the same and pay out of the proceeds the claims of A's creditors. A reserves no power of revocation. If no communication has been made to the creditors, A may revoke the trust. But if the creditors are parties to the arrangement, the trust cannot be revoked without their consent.

79. Revocation not to defeat what trustees have duly done

No trust can be revoked by the author of the trust so as to defeat or prejudice what the trustees may have duly done in execution of the trust.

CHAPTER IX : OF CERTAIN OBLIGATIONS IN THE NATURE OF TRUSTS

80. Where obligation in nature of trust is created

An obligation in the nature of a trust is created in the following cases.

81. Where it does not appear that transferor intended to dispose of beneficial interest

[4][***]

82. Transfer to one for consideration paid by another]

[4][***]

83. Trust incapable of execution or executed without exhausting trust-property

Where a trust is incapable of being executed, or where the trust is completely executed without exhausting the trust-property, the trustee, in the absence of a direction to the contrary, must hold the trust-property, or so much thereof as is unexhausted, for the benefit of the author of the trust or his legal representative.

Illustrations

(a) A conveys certain land to B-

"upon trust", and no trust is declared; or

"upon trust to be thereafter declared", and no such declaration is ever made; or

upon trusts that are too vague to be executed; or

upon trusts that become incapable of taking effect; or

"in trust for C", and C renounces his interest under the trust. In each of these cases B holds the land for the benefit of A.

(b) A transfers Rs. 10,000 in the four per cents to B, in trust to pay the interest annually accruing due to C for her life. A dies. Then C dies. B holds the funds for the benefit of A's legal representative.

(c) A conveys land to B upon trust to sell it and apply one moiety of the proceeds for certain charitable purposes, and the other for the maintenance of the worship of an idol. B sells the land, but the charitable purposes wholly fail, and the maintenance of the worship does not exhaust the second moiety of the proceeds. B holds the first moiety and the part unapplied of the second moiety for the benefit of A or his legal representative.

(d) A bequeaths Rs. 10,000 to B, to be laid out in buying land to be conveyed for purposes with either wholly or partially fail to take effect. B holds for the benefit of A's legal representative the undisposed of interest in the money or land if purchased.

84. Transfer for illegal purpose

Where the owner of property transfers it to another for an illegal purpose and such purpose is not carried into execution, or the transferor is not as guilty as the transferee, or the effect of permitting the transferee to retain the property might be to defeat the provisions of any law, the transferee must hold the property for the benefit of the transferor.

85. Bequest for illegal purpose

Where a testator bequeaths certain property upon trust

and the purpose of the trust appears on the face of the will to be unlawful, or during the testator's lifetime the legatee agrees with him to apply the property for an unlawful purpose, legatee must hold the property for the benefit of the testator's legal representative.

Bequest of which revocation is prevented by coercion: Where property is bequeathed and the revocation of the bequest is prevented by coercion, the legatee must hold the property for the benefit of the testator's legal representative.

86. Transfer pursuant to rescindable contract

Where property is transferred in pursuance of contract which is liable to rescission or induced by fraud or mistake, the transferee must, on receiving notice to that effect, hold the property for the benefit of the transferor, subject to repayment by the latter of the consideration actually paid.

87. Debtor becoming creditor's representative

Where a debtor becomes the executor or other legal representative of his creditor, he must hold the debt for the benefit of the persons interested therein.

88. Advantage gained by fiduciary

Where a trustee, executor, partner, agent, director of a company, legal advisor, or other person bound in a fiduciary character to protect the interests of another person, by availing himself of his character, gains for himself any pecuniary advantage, or where any person, so bound enters into any dealings under circumstances in which his own interests are, or may be, adverse to those of such other person and thereby gains for himself a pecuniary advantage, he must hold for the benefit of such other person the advantage so gained.

Illustrations

(a) A, an executor, buys at an undervalue from B, a legatee, his claim under the will, B is ignorant of the value of the bequest. A must hold for the benefit of B the difference between the price and value.

(b) A, a trustee, uses the trust-property for the purpose of his own business. A holds for the benefit of his beneficiary the profits arising from such user.

(c) A, a trustee, retires from his trust in consideration of his successor paying him a sum of money. A holds such money for the benefit of his beneficiary.

(d) A, a partner, buys land in his own name with funds belonging to the partnership. A holds such land for the benefit of the partnership.

(e) A, a partner, employed on behalf of himself and his co-partners is negotiating the terms of a lease, clandestinely stipulates with the lessor for payment to himself of a lakh of rupees. A holds the lakh for the benefit of the partnership.

(f) A and B are partners. A dies. B, instead of winding up the affairs of the partnership, retain all the assets in the business. B must account to A's legal representative for the profits arising from A's share of the capital.

(g) A, an agent employed to obtain a lease for B, obtains the lease for himself. A holds the lease for the benefit of B.

(h) A, a guardian, buys up for himself incumbrances on his ward B's estate at an undervalue. A holds for the benefit of B the incumbrances so bought, and can only charge him with what he has actually paid.

89. Advantage gained by exercise of undue influence

Where, by the exercise of undue influence, any advantage is gained in derogation of the interests of another, the person gaining such advantage without consideration, or with notice that such influence has been exercised, must hold the advantage for the benefit of the person whose interests have been so prejudiced.

90. Advantage gained by qualified owner

Where a tenant for life, co-owner, mortgagee or other qualified owner of any property by availing himself of his position as such, gains an advantage in derogation of the rights of the other persons interested in the property, or where any such owner, as representing all persons interested in such property, gains any advantage, he must hold, for the benefit of all persons so interested, the advantage so gained, but subject to repayment by such persons of their due share of the expenses properly incurred, and to an indemnity by the same persons against liabilities properly contracted, in gaining such advantage.

Illustrations

(a) A, the tenant for life of leasehold property, renews the lease in his own name and for his own benefit. A holds the renewed lease for the benefit of all those interested in the old lease.

(b) A village belongs to a Hindu family. A, one of its members, pays nazrana to government and thereby procures his name to be entered as the inamdar of the village. A holds the village for the benefit of himself and the other members.

(c) A mortgages land to B, who enters into possession. B allows the government revenue to fall into arrear

with a view to the land being put up for sale and his becoming himself the purchaser of it. The land is accordingly sold to B. Subject to the repayment of the amount due on the mortgage and of his expenses properly incurred as mortgagee, B holds the land for the benefit of A.

91. Property acquired with notice of existing contract

Where a person acquires property with notice that another person has entered into an existing contract affecting that property, of which specified performance could be enforced, the former must hold the property for the benefit of the latter to the extent necessary to give effect to the contract.

92. Purchase by person contracting to buy property to be held on trust

Where a person contracts to buy property to be held on trust for certain beneficiaries and buys the property accordingly, he must hold the property for their benefit to the extent necessary to give effect to the contract.

93. Advantage secretly gained by one of several compounding creditors

Where creditors compound the debts due to them, and one of such creditors, by a secret arrangement with the debtor, gains an undue advantage over his co-creditors, he must hold for the benefit of such creditors the advantage so gained.

94. Constructive trusts in cases not expressly provided for

[4][* * *]

95. Obligor's duties, liabilities and disabilities

The person holding property in accordance with any of the preceding sections of this chapter must, so far as may be, perform the same duties, and is subject, so far as may be, to the same liabilities and disabilities, as if he were a trustee of the property for the person for whose benefit he holds it:

Provided that, (a) where he rightfully cultivates the property or employs it in trade or business, he is entitled to reasonable remuneration for his trouble, skill and loss of time in such cultivation or employment; and (b) where he holds the property by virtue of a contract with the person for whose benefit he holds it, or with anyone through whom such person claims, he may, without the permission of the court, by or become lessee or mortgagee of the property or any part thereof.

96. Saving of rights of bona fide purchasers

Nothing contained in this Chapter shall impair the rights of transferees in good faith for consideration, or create an obligation in evasion of any law for the time being in force.

APPENDIX—4

LIST OF INTERNATIONAL NGOS

1 Action Against Hunger
875 Ave of the Americas,
Suite 1905
New York, NY 10001

2 ADRA International
Earthquake Relief-India
12501 Old Columbia Pike
Silver Spring, MD 20904

3 American Friends Service Committee (AFSC)
India Earthquake Relief & Reconstruction Fund
1501 Cherry Street
Philadelphia, PA 19102

4. American Jewish Joint Distribution Committee
India Earthquake Relief
711 Third Avenue
10th Floor New York, New York 10017

5 American Jewish World Service
India Earthquake Relief
989 Avenue of the Americas
10th Floor New York, NY 10018

6 American Red Cross
International Response Fund
PO Box 37243
Washington, DC 20013

7 Ananda Marga Universal Relief Teams (AMURT)
"AMURT India Quake"
7627 16th Street, NW
Washington, DC 20012

8 Baptist World Aid
Indian Earthquake Appeal
6733 Curran Street
McLean, VA 22101

9 B'nai B'rith International
Disaster Relief - India Earthquake
2640 Rhode Island Avenue, NW
Washington,DC 20036

10 Brother's Brother Foundation
India Earthquake
Suite 3005, 1501 Reedsdale Street
Pittsburgh, PA 15233

11 CARE
151 Ellis St, NE
Atlanta, GA 30303
(800) 521-CARE

12 Catholic Medical Mission Board
10 West 17th St.
New York, NY 10011
(800) 678-5659, ext. 18

13 Catholic Relief Services
India Earthquake Fund
PO Box 17090
Baltimore, MD 21203-7090

14 Christian Children's Fund
India Earthquake
PO Box 26484
Richmond, VA 23261

15 Christian Reformed World Relief Committee
India Earthquake
2850 Kalamazoo Avenue SE
Grand Rapids, MI 49560

16 Church World Service
India Earthquake
PO Box 968
Elkhart, IN 46515

17 Concern Worldwide US
Suite 903
104 east 40th Street
New York, NY 10016

18 Counterpart International
Attn: Nina Anlauf
1200 18th Street NW, Suite 1100
Washington, DC. 20036

19 Direct Relief International
mark check "India"
27 South La Patera Lane
Santa Barbara, CA 93117

20 Episcopal Relief & Development
Earthquake Relief-India
Box 12043
Newark, NJ 07101

21 Food for the Hungry
7729 E.Greenway Road
Scottsdale, AZ 85260
(800) 2-HUNGER

22 Heart to Heart International
Disaster Relief Fund
401 S.Clairborne, Ste. 302
Olathe, KS 66062

23 International Aid
17011 W. Hickory
Spring Lake, MI 49456
(800) 251-2502

24 International Relief Teams
C/o India Earthquake Relief
3547 Camino Del Rio South, #C
San Diego, CA 92108

25 Latter-day Saint Charities
50 E North Temple Street
7th Floor
Salt Lake City, UT 84150

26 Lutheran World Relief
India Earthquake
PO Box 17061
Baltimore, MD 21298

27 MAP International
Emergency Relief Fund
PO Box 215000
Brunswick, GA 31521

28 Mercy Corps International
India Earthquake Relief, Dept. NR.
PO Box 2669
Portland, OR 97208-2669

29 Mercy-USA for Aid & Development
Attn: India Earthquake Relief
44450 Pinetree Dr. Ste. 201
Plymouth, MI 48170-3869

30 Northwest Medical Teams International
PO Box 10
Portland, Oregon 97207
(503) 624-1000

31 Operation USA
mark check "India"
8320 Melrose Avenue
Los Angeles, CA 90069

32 Oxfam America
India Earthquake Response
PO Box 1745
Boston, MA 02105

33 Relief International
11965 Venice Blvd. #405
Los Angeles, CA 90066
(310) 572-7770

34 Save the Children
PO Box 975-India Earthquake
Westport, CT 06881
(800) 728-3843

35 United Methodist Committee On Relief
mark donation "India" Earthquake Advance #274305-0"
475 Riverside Dr., Room 330
New York, NY 10115

36 US Fund for UNICEF
333 East 38th Street
New York, NY 10016
(800) FOR-KIDS

37 United Way International
701 North Fairfax Street
Alexandria, VA 22314
(703) 519-0092

38 World Concern
19303 Fremont Avenue North
Seattle, WA 98133
(800) 755-5022

39 World Relief
Dept.3
PO Box WRC
Wheaton, IL 60189

40 World Vision
India Quake Relief
PO Box 70288
Tacoma, WA 98481

41 YMCA World Service
National YMCA Fund, Inc.
101 N.Wacker Dr.
Chicago, IL 60606

APPENDIX—5

SOCIETIES REGISTRATION ACT, 1860

[Act No. 21 of Yr. 1860]

An Act for the registration of literary, scientific and charitable societies

Whereas it is expedient the provision should be made for improving the legal condition or societies established for the promotion of literature, science, or the fine arts, or for the diffusion of useful knowledge, [1][the diffusion of political education], or for charitable purposes;

It is enacted as follows :-

1. Societies formed by memorandum of association and registration

Any seven or more persons associated for any literary, scientific, or charitable purpose, or for any such purpose as is described in section 20 of this Act, may, by subscribing their names to a memorandum of association, and filing the same with Registrar of Joint-stock Companies [2][***] form themselves into a society under this Act.

2. Memorandum of association

The memorandum of association shall contain the following things, that is to say,-

the name of the society;

the object of the society;

the names, addresses, and occupations of the governors, council, directors, committee, or other governing body to whom, by the rules of the society, the management of its affairs is entrusted.

A copy of the rules and regulations of the society, certified to be a correct copy by not less than three of the members of the governing body, shall be filed with the memorandum of association.

3. Registration and fees

Upon such memorandum and certified copy being filed, the Registrar shall certify under his hand that the society is registered under this Act. There shall be paid to the Registrar for every such registration a fee of fifty rupees, or such smaller fees as [3][the State Government] may from time to time, direct; and all fees so paid shall be accounted for to [3][the State Government].

4. Annual list of managing body to be filed

Once in every year, on or before the fourteenth day succeeding the day on which, according to the rules of the society, the annual general meeting of the societies is held, or, if it rules do not provide for an annual general meeting, in the months of January, list shall be filed with the Registrar of Joint Stock Companies, of the names, addresses and occupations of the governors, council, director, committee, or other governing body then entrusted with the management of the affairs of the society.

5. Property of society how vested

The property, movable and immovable belonging to a society registered under this Act, if not vested in trustees, shall be deemed to be vested, for the time being, in the governing body of such society, and in all proceedings civil and criminal, may be described as the property of the governing body of such society for their proper title.

6. Suits by and against societies

Every society registered under this Act may sue or be sued in the name of President, Chairman, or Principal Secretary, or trustees, as shall be determined by the rules and regulations of the society and, in default of such determination, in the name of such person as shall be appointed by the governing body for the occasion:

Provided that it shall be competent for any person having a claim, or demand against the society, to sue the President or Chairman, or Principal Secretary or the trustees thereof, if on application the governing body some other officer or person be not nominated to be the defendant.

7. Suits not to abate

No suit or proceeding in any Civil Court shall abate or discontinue by reason of the person, by or against whom such suit or proceedings shall have been brought or continued, dying or ceasing to fill the character in the name whereof he shall have sued or been sued, but the same suit proceedings shall be continued in the name of or against the successor of such person.

8. Enforcement of judgment against society

If a judgment shall be recovered against the person or officer named on behalf of the society, such judgment shall not be put in force against the property, movable or immovable, or against the body of such person or officer, but against the property of the society.

The application for execution shall set forth the judgement, the fact of the party against whom it shall have been recovered having sued or having been sued, as the case may be, on behalf of the society only, and shall require to have the judgement enforced against the property of the society.

9. Recovery of penalty accruing under bye-law

Whenever by any bye-law duly made in accordance with the rules and regulations of the society, or, if the rules do not provide for the making of bye-laws, by any bye-laws made at a general meeting of the members of the society convened for the purpose (for the making of which the concurrent votes of three-fifths of the members present at such meeting shall be necessary), any pecuniary penalty is imposed for the breach of any rule or bye-law of the society, such penalty, when accrued, may be recovered in any court having jurisdiction where the defendant shall reside, or the society shall be situate, as the governing body thereof shall deem expedient.

10. Members liable to be sued as strangers

Any member who may be in arrear of a subscription which according to the rules of the society he is bound to pay, or who shall possess himself of or detain any property of the society in a manner or for a time contrary to such rules, or shall injure or destroy any property of the society, may be sued for such arrear or for the damage accruing from such detention, injury, or destruction of the property in the manner hereinbefore provided.

Recovery by successful defendant of costs adjudged : But if the defendant shall be successful in any suit or other proceedings brought against him at the instance of the society, and shall be adjudged to recover his costs, he may elect to proceed to recover the same from the officer in whose name the suit shall be brought, or from the society, and in the latter case shall have process against the property of the said society in the manner above described.

11. Members guilty of offences punishable as strangers

Any member of the society who shall steal, purloin, or embezzle any money or other property, or wilfully, and maliciously destroy or injure any property of such society, or shall forge and deed, bond, security for money, receipt, or other instrument, whereby the funds of the society may be exposed to loss, shall be subject to the same prosecution, and, if convicted, shall be liable to be punished in like manner, as any person not a member would be subject and liable to in respect of the like offence.

12. Societies enabled to alter, extend or abridge their purposes

Whenever it shall appear to the governing body of any society registered under this Act, which has been established for any particular purpose or purposes, that it is advisable to alter, extend, or abridge such purpose to or for other purposes within the meaning of this Act, or to amalgamate such society either wholly or partially with any other society, such governing body may submit the proposition to the members of the society in a written or printed report, and may convene a special meeting for the consideration thereof according to the regulations of the society;

> but no such proposition shall be carried into effect unless such report shall have been delivered or sent by post to every member of the society ten days previous to the special meeting convened by the governing body for the consideration thereof, nor unless such proposition shall have been agreed to by the votes of three-fifths of the members delivered in person or by proxy, and confirmed by the votes of three-fifths of the

members present at a second special meeting convened by the governing body at an interval of one months after the former meeting.

13. Provision for dissolution of societies and adjustment of their affairs

Any number not less than three-fifths of the members of any society may determine that it shall be dissolved, and thereupon it shall be dissolved forthwith, or at the time then agreed upon, and all necessary steps shall be taken for the disposal and settlement of the property of the society, its claims and liabilities according to the rules of the said society applicable thereto, if any, and if not, then as the governing body shall find expedient, provided that, in the event of any dispute arising among the said governing body or the members of the society, the adjustment of its affairs shall be referred to the principal court of original civil jurisdiction of the district in which the chief building of the society is situate; and the court shall make such order in the matter as it shall deem requisite.

Assent required: Provided that no societies shall be dissolved unless three-fifths of the members shall have expressed a wish for dissolution by their votes delivered in person, or by proxy, at a general meeting convened for the purpose:

Government consent: Provided that [4][whenever any Government] is a member of, or a contributor to, or otherwise interested in any society registered under this Act, such society shall not be dissolved [5][without the consent of the Government of the [6][State] or registration].

14. Upon a dissolution no member to receive profit

If upon the dissolution of any society registered under

this Act there shall remain, after the satisfaction of all its debts and liabilities, any property whatsoever, the same shall not be paid to or distributed among the members of the said society or any of them, but shall be given to some other society, to be determined by the votes of not less than three-fifths of the members present personally or by proxy at the time of the dissolution, or in default thereof, by such court as aforesaid:

Clause not to apply to Joint-stock Companies : Provided, however, that this clause shall not apply to any society which has been founded or established by the contributions of share-holders in the nature of a Joint-stock Company.

15. Member defined

For the purposes of this Act a member of a society shall be a person who, having been admitted therein according to the rules and regulations thereof, shall have paid a subscription, or shall have signed the roll or list of members thereof, and shall not have resigned in accordance with such rules and regulations;

Disqualified members : But in all proceedings under this Act no person shall be entitled to vote or be counted as a member whose subscription at the time shall have been in arrears for a period exceeding three months.

16. Governing body defined

The governing body of the society shall be the governors, council, directors, committee, trustees, or other body to whom by the rules and regulations of the society the management of its affairs is entrusted.

17. Registration of societies formed before Act

Any company or society established for a literary,

scientific or charitable purpose, and registered under Act 43 of 1850[7], or any such society established and constituted previously to the passing of this Act but not registered under the said Act 43 of 1850 may at any time hereafter be registered as a society under this Act.

Assent required : Subject to the proviso that no such company or society shall be registered under this Act unless an assent to its being so registered has been given by three-fifths of the members present personally, or by proxy, at some general meeting convened for that purpose by the governing body.

In the case of a company or society registered under this Act 43 of 1850[7], the directors shall be deemed to be such governing body.

In the case of a society not so registered, if no such body shall have been constituted on the establishment of the society, it shall be competent for the members thereof, upon due notice, to create for itself a governing body to act for the society thenceforth.

18. Such societies to file memorandum, etc. with Registrar of Joint-stock Companies

In order to any such society as is mentioned in the last proceeding section obtaining registry under this Act, it shall be sufficient that the governing body file with the Registrar of Joint-stock Companies [2][* * *] a memorandum showing the name of the society, the objects of the society, and the names, addresses and occupations of the governing body, together with a copy of the rules and regulations of the society certified as provided in section 2, and a copy of the report of the proceedings of the general meeting at which the registration was resolved on.

19. Inspection of documents

Any person may inspect all documents filed with the Registrar under this Act on payment of a fee of one rupee for each inspection; and any person may require a copy or extract of any document or any part of any document, to be certified by the registrar, on payment of two annas for every hundred words of such copy or extract; and such certified copy shall be prima facie evidence of the matters therein contained in all legal proceedings whatever.

20. To what societies Act applies

The following societies may be registered under this Act:-

Charitable societies, the military orphan funds or societies established at the several presidencies of India, societies established for the promotion of science, literature, or the fine arts for instruction, the diffusion of useful knowledge, [1][the diffusion of political education], the foundation or maintenance of libraries or reading-rooms for general use among the members or open to the public or public museums and galleries of paintings and other works of art, collections of natural history, mechanical and philosophical inventions, instruments, or designs.

NOTES

1. Inserted by Act 22 of 1927.
2. Phrase "under Act No. 19 of 1857" omitted by Act 16 of 1874.
3. Substituted by the Adaptation of Laws Order, 1950, for the phrase "provincial Government".
4. Substituted by the Adaptation of Indian Laws Order, 1937, for the words "whenever the Government".
5. Substituted by the Adaptation of Indian Laws Orders, 1937, for the phrase "without the consent of the Government of state of Registration".

6. Substituted by the Adaptation of Laws Order, 1950, for the word "Province".
7. Act No. 43 of 1850 which is the Joint Stock Companies Act, 1850 stands repealed by s. 219 of Indian Companies Act, 1866 (10 of 1866) which was also repealed by the Companies Act, 1956.

Glossary

Accredited: This is being officially recognized as an organization affiliated with the United Nations.

Agenda 21: A document adopted by UNCED as a program of action on sustainable development for all sectors of government and society in each country.

Attitudes: Personal biases, preferences, and subjective assessments that predispose one to act or respond in a predictable manner. Attitudes lead people to like or dislike something, or to consider things good or bad, important or unimportant, worth caring about or not worth caring about.

Caucus: A term derived from politics in the USA, meaning a group of people who meet together to devise a common political strategy.

Child-friendly designs: Technical designs that take into account that facilities will be used by children and adapt the facilities to children's skills and abilities to use them.

Civil society: A complex contested term, usually referring to all people, their activities and their relationships that are not part of the process of government. It may also be used to cover all processes other than government and economic activity.

Commission on the Status of Women: The United Nations Commission on the Status of Women, established in 1946 as a functional commission of the Economic and Social Council, has, as its objective, the promotion of equal rights between men and women. Following the Fourth World Conference on Women, the General Assembly further mandated it to integrate into its work a follow-up process to the Conference. In that context, the Commission should play a catalytic role regularly reviewing the critical areas of concern in the Beijing Platform for Action. The Commission consists of 45 members elected by the Council for four years. Members, who are appointed by governments, are elected on the following basis: 13 from African States; 11 from Asian States; four from Eastern European States; nine from Latin American and the Caribbean States; and eight from Western European and Other States. The Commission normally meets annually.

Conference: In the context of the United Nations, a conference is an official international meeting planned to study some specific question. The latest cycle of conferences included the Cairo Population Conference in 1994, the Copenhagen Social Summit in 1995, the Fourth World Conference on Women in 1995, the Environment Conference, Habitat II, in Istanbul in 1996.

CONGO: FAWCO is a member of the Conference Of Non-Governmental Organizations in Consultative Relationship with the United Nations (CONGO) is an independent, international, not-for-profit membership association of NGOs that facilitates their participation in United Nations debates and decisions. CONGO is most active in the major UN centers of New York, Geneva, and Vienna, but extends its work to all regions of the world. CONGO's major objective is to ensure that NGOs are present when governments discuss issues of global concern at the United Nations and to facilitate NGO discussions on such issues. CONGO's membership comprises national, regional and international nongovernmental organizations in consultative status with the United Nations Economic and Social Council (ECOSOC). Their broad membership email-network has become a major source of information for NGOs active within the United Nations and seeking collaboration/partnerships with other NGOs of similar concerns. For more information visit their website at www.ngocongo.org or email congo@ngocongo.org.

Consultative Status: NGOs may be admitted into a mutually beneficial working relationship with the United Nations by attaining consultative status with the Economic and Social Council (ECOSOC). This status is based on Article 71 of the Charter of the United Nations and on ECOSOC resolution1996/31, adopted in 1996. The rights and privileges, enable qualifying organizations to make a contribution to the work programs and goals of the United Nations by serving as technical experts, advisers and consultants to governments and Secretariat. Sometimes, as advocacy groups, they espouse UN themes, implementing plans of action, programs and declarations adopted by the United Nations. In concrete terms this entails their participation in ECOSOC and its various subsidiary bodies through attendance at these meetings, and also through oral interventions and written statements on agenda items of those bodies. In addition, organizations, qualifying for General Category consultative status, may propose new items for consideration by the ECOSOC. Organizations granted status are also invited to attend international conferences called by the UN, General Assembly special sessions, and other intergovernmental bodies.

Consultative status: The arrangements specified in three resolutions of ECOSOC in 1950, 1968 and 1996, whereby NGOs may be given the right to participate in ECOSOC and all its subsidiary bodies.

Cost recovery: The degree to which the costs of water supply and sanitation services are paid for by the users. Includes two categories of costs: the initial investment costs and the continuous cost of operation and maintenance. The basic cost recovery principle requires that 100 percent of operation and maintenance costs be covered by the users. As for the initial investment costs, users are usually required to pay a part of them, possibly through in-kind contributions made by the parents.

CSD: UN Commission on Sustainable Development, reporting to ECOSOC, the most important intergovernmental policy-making body on environmental questions. Its influence is through the impact on the policy of governments. It has no programs of its own.

DPI: The Department of Public Information of the United Nations has its headquarters in New York, and has as its mission diffusion of United Nations news to accredited member organizations. The DPI was the first UN branch to officially accredit FAWCO to its list of members in July, 1995.

ECOSOC: Economic and Social Council of the United Nations: one of the 'principal organs' specified in the UN Charter and the body to which NGOs are accredited.

ECOSOC: The Economic and Social Council of the United Nations deals with economic and social questions, as its name implies. FAWCO was given special consultative status with ECOSOC in August 1997. There are currently 2012 NGOs in consultative status with the Economic and Social Council. These organizations have the privilege and opportunity to submit opinions to the Council and the responsibility to submit a report once every four years detailing their activities in support of the UN. (Read FAWCO's Report to ECOSOC for 1997 to 2001. The 54-member Economic and Social Council serves as the central forum for discussing international economic and social issues, and for formulating policy recommendations addressed to Member States and to the United Nations. It makes or initiates studies and reports; makes recommendations on international economic, social, cultural, educational, health and related matters; and promotes respect for, and observance of, human rights and fundamental freedoms. Subsidiary bodies, commissions and committees of ECOSOC carry out its year-round work. ECOSOC strengthens cooperation within the UN system, coordinates the work of the specialized agencies and consults with non-governmental organizations. A substantive session of the Council is convened annually in July, and supplementary formal meetings as well as informal panels on topical issues are held throughout the year.

Enabling Environment: Attitudes, policies, and practices that stimulate and support effective and efficient functioning of organizations and individuals.

Financial Policy: If inadequate attention is given to cost recovery issues, operations and maintenance are likely to be compromised. Establishing and enforcing effective financial policies is an essential, but often poorly practiced, element of implementing successful demand-responsive approaches. An adequate financial policy is built on these basic principles: (i) Users should pay for services, since experience shows that commitment of user resources demonstrates the value the service; (ii) Ideally, users should pay the full cost of investment and operation and maintenance costs. If the government applies a subsidy for service delivery, it should. follow these rules: (a) An explicit per-school subsidy may be the most efficient; (b) The subsidy should be set below the per-school average for the most basic level of service; (c) If higher levels of service are demanded, users should pay the incremental costs beyond the basic service level.

Gender: Concerns roles and relationships of women and men, including how they cooperate and share work, make decisions, and exercise control in projects and programs. Projects must identify and address these differences and interrelationships to ensure that both men and women have the resources they require for their development.

Hygiene Promotion: A planned approach that identifies environmental and health problems caused by poor sanitation and subsequently changes behavior among students and in the community by encouraging the widespread adoption of safe hygiene practices. It is a long-term process and should form part of the general work program of Ministries of Education and Health.

INGO: International non-governmental organization.

Life Skills: Abilities for adaptive and positive behavior that enable individuals to deal effectively with the demands and challenges of everyday life. In particular, life skills are a group of psychosocial competencies and interpersonal skills that help people make informed decisions, solve problems, think critically and creatively, communicate effectively, build healthy relationships, empathize with others, and cope with and manage their lives in a hygienic, healthy, and productive manner.

Life Skills-based Hygiene Education: An approach to creating and maintaining hygienic lifestyles and conditions through the development of knowledge, attitudes, and especially skills, using a variety of learning experiences, with an emphasis on participatory methods. It should enable a child to make positive decisions and take actions to promote and protect health and hygienic conditions for themselves and for others.

Major Group: One of a list of nine categories of NGOs specified in *Agenda 21*.

Millennium Development Goals: In September 2000, world leaders at the Millennium Summit agreed on an ambitious agenda for reducing poverty and improving lives. This ambition was formulated in eight Millennium Development Goals. For each goal one or more targets were set, most to be achieved by 2015, using 1990 as a benchmark. Three goals are relevant for hygiene, sanitation, and water in schools: achieve universal primary education, promote gender equality and empower women, and ensure environmental sustainability.

Monitoring and Evaluation: Monitoring is observation of how a project is implemented and operates; it provides timely information for ensuring that progress, quality, and effect of processes and procedures are maintained. Evaluation focuses on whether a project is being implemented as intended, examines how the project operates, and addresses problems in service delivery.

National NGO: An NGO based in one country. It is a misnomer as most countries are multi-national, but use of this standard term cannot be avoided.

Network: A coalition of NGOs and/or individual people, at the minimum sharing information and at the maximum devising a common political strategy. Use of the term implies the relationships are loose and informal.

NGO Forum: Each official United Nations Conference has been accompanied by an NGO Forum, which is where the real interest and work is done. The Forums offer an opportunity to meet and network with people from every country and every sort of organization, all of whom are working to bring about change in the world, from whatever perspective. In addition, the NGO Forums prepare a statement which is presented to the official UN meeting, and which can and often does actually influence the content of the official paper written by conference members.

NGO: Any non-governmental organization, big or small, international or local, which is permitted to participate in United Nations related activities as stated in Chapter 10 Article 71 of the United Nations Charter. The term NGO covers a range of organizations, as large as Amnesty International, Green Peace, "Medecins du Monde" - or as small as a community organization. The largest NGO, the Red Cross has 105 million members. The term originated as a means of distinguishing organizations which might take part in international or UN-related activities, and which were NOT sponsored by any government from those which ARE government-sponsored. FAWCO has been recognized as an NGO by the United Nations since 1995.

Observer Status: As the name implies, observers do not participate in debate nor help to shape policies drafted at official meetings.

Platform for Action: The official paper which came out of the Beijing Conference is called the "Platform for Action". It has 12 principal points to be worked on in connection with women's interests: Health, Violence, Armed Conflict, Economy, Decision Making, Institutional Mechanisms, Human Rights, Media, Environment, the Girl-Child, Poverty, Educational Training. Many of these are topics have long been addressed by FAWCO.

Program Communication: The process of identifying, segmenting, and targeting specific groups and audiences with particular strategies, messages, or training programs; it involves reaching them through various mass media and interpersonal channels, both traditional and non-traditional.

Project Cycle: Systematizes the interactive process between the project and the school, with additional input and support provided by national and local government, parents, community, NGOs, the private sector, and other possible stakeholders.

School Hygiene Committee: A working committee for decisionmaking, financial oversight, and management of water supply, sanitation, and hand washing facilities. The committee is also responsible for the supervision of health, hygiene, and sanitation aspects related to water consumption.

SMART Objectives: Objectives that are defined by five characteristics: Specific, Measurable, Available at an acceptable cost, Relevant, and Time-bound. Such objectives also form the basis for a future monitoring and evaluation system.

Social Intermediation: A process that enables school communities to carry out collective action for the selection, implementation, maintenance, and sustainability of hygiene, water supply, and sanitation in schools. It has two objectives: to enable school communities to make informed choices about collective investment decisions, and to provide training that will enable school communities to plan, implement, and manage hygiene, water supply, and sanitation services.

Social Movement: A large number of people who challenge established social norms and express themselves through a variety of forms of mass social and/or political action.

Transnational: Any relationship across country boundaries, in which at least one of the actors is not a government. Most commonly applied to companies, but only when they go beyond trade, to own or control branches, subsidiaries or affiliates in more than one country.

Umbrella group: A coalition of NGOs operating in different fields, in a more formal, structured arrangement than a network.

UNCED: United Nations Conference on Environment and Development, 3-14 June 1992, held in Rio de Janeiro: popularly know as the Earth Summit.

Bibliography

Abdulhadi, Nural. *The Kuwaiti NGOs: Their Role in Aid Flows to Developing Countries.* Working Paper Series 524. Washington: The World Bank, Policy and Review Department, October 1990.

Alex Inkles, "Participant Citizenship in Six Developing Countries," *The American Political Science Review,* Vol. LXIII, No. 4, 1969, p. 1122.

Almond, Gabriel and Verba, Sidney, *The Civic Culture,* Boston, Little Brown, p. 161.

Anthony, M. Orum, *Introduction to Political Sociology,* New Jersey, Prentice Hall Inc., Englewood, p. 308.

Aronson, Dan, *Participation in Country Economic and Sector Work.* Paper prepared for the World Bank Workshop on Participatory Development, May 1994.

Arya, Ved (1996). *Towards a Relationship of Significance.* New Delhi: PRADAN.

Asian NGO Coalition for Agrarian Reform and Rural Development (ANGOC). 1988. "NGOs and International Development Cooperation." Lok Niti 5(4).

Aufderheide, Pat and Bruce Rich. "Environmental Reform and the Multilateral Banks", in *World Policy Journal*, Spring 1988.

B. Chowdhary, D.P. (1979): Social Welfare Administration, Atma Ram and Sons, New Delhi, p. 20.

Baile, Stephanie. *Survey of European Nongovernmental Aid Organizations: A Guide to NGOs and their Perception of the World Bank.* Paris: World Bank, May 1986.

Basu, Amrita (1992). *Two faces of Protest: Contrasting Modes of Women's Activism in India* Berkeley: University of California Press.

Bebbington, Anthony and John Farrington. 1992a. "Private Voluntary Initiatives: Enhancing the Public Sector's Capacity to Respond to Nongovernmental Organization Needs." Paper presented at the Twelfth Agricultural Sector Symposium, World Bank, January 8.

Bebbington, Anthony et.al. *Nongovernmental Organizations and the State in Latin America.* London: Routledge, 1993.

Beckmann, David. "Recent Experience and Emerging Trends" in Samuel Paul and Israel Arturo, *NGOs and the World Bank: Cooperation for Development.* Washington: World Bank, 1992.

Bhatnagar, Bhuvan and Aubrey Williams. *Participatory Development and the World Bank: Potential Directions for Change.* World Bank Discussion Paper No. 183. Washington: World Bank, 1992.

Bhatnagar, Bhuvan. *Non-Governmental Organizations and World Bank- Supported Projects in Asia: Lessons Learned.* Departmental Papers Series No. 2. Washington: World Bank, Asia Technical Department, May 1991.

Bhatt, Anil (1995). 'Voluntary action in India', *Economic and Political Weekly,* Vol. 30, No. 16, pp. 870-76.

Bonner, Arthur (1990). *Averting the Apocalypse: Social Movements in India Today*. Durham: Duke University Press.

Boyer, David. *The Role of Northern NGOs in the Promotion of Sustainable Development in Africa*. Edinburgh: Centre of African Studies, 1990.

Bratton, Michael. "The Politics of Government: NGO Relations in Africa", in *World Development*. Vol. 17, No. 4, 1989. pp. 569-587.

Brautigam, Deborah. 1991. "Development, Institutional Pluralism and the Voluntary Sector." Paper for World Bank, EXTIE. Washington, D.C.

Brodhead, Tim, Brent Herbert-Copley, and Anne-Marie Lambert. *Bridges of Hope? Canadian Voluntary Agencies and the Third World*. Ottawa: The North-South Institute, 1988.

Brown, David and David Korten. *Understanding Voluntary Organizations: Guidelines for Donors*. Working Paper 258. Washington: World Bank, Country Economics Department, September 1989.

Brown, L. David. 1988. "Organizational Barriers to NGO Strategic Action." Lok Niti 5(4).

Bryce, Lord in Constance Smith and Ann Freedom, *Voluntary Associations; Perspectives on the Literature*, Cambridge (Mass) Harvard University Press, 1972.

C.E. Black, *The Dynamics of Modernization*, New York, Harper and Row Publishers, Inc. 1966, pp. 13-18.

C.P. Bhambhri, "Administration and Citizen in India: An Analytical and Perspective Profile", *Indian Journal of Public Administration*, Vol. XXI, July'-Sep. 1995, p. 338.

Calman, Leslie J. (1992). *Toward Empowerment: Women and Movement Politics in India.* Boulder, CO: Westview Press, pp. 21-46.

Canaan Ram A., Felice D. Perlmutter and Chul-Hei Kang (1991). 'Voluntary associations: Societal variations in response to human needs', paper presented at the Third International Conference of Research on Voluntary and Nonprofit Organizations, Indianapolis, 11-13 March, p. 1.

Carroll, Tom. *Intermediary NGOs*. Washington: Inter-American Foundation, 1992.

Carvalho, Soniya, *Social Funds: Guidelines for Design and Implementation*, ESP Discussion Paper Series No. 24. Washington: World Bank, March 1994

Cernea, Michael M. *Nongovernmental Organizations and Local Development*. Discussion Paper No. 10. Washington: World Bank, 1988.

Chambers, Robert (1995). 'Poverty and livelihood: Whose reality counts', IDS discussion paper, Sussex, December.

Chambers, Robert. 1983. Rural Development: Putting the Last First. Harlow: Longman.

Chowdhary, D.P. (1971): voluntary Social Welfare in India, Sterling Publisher Ltd, Delhi, p. 54.

Clark, John (1991). *Democratizing Development: The Role of Voluntary Organizations,* London: Earthscan Publications.

Clark, John. *Democratizing Development: The Role of Voluntary Organizations*. London: Earthscan Publications, 1991

Clark, John. *The State and the Voluntary Sector.* Human

Resources and Operations Policy Working Paper No. 12. Washington: World Bank, October 1993.

Clark, Peter B..and James Q. Wilson (1961). 'Incentive systems: A theory of organizations', *Administrative Science Quarterly* 6, pp. 129-66.

Daniel Lerner, *The Passing of Traditional Society,* Glencoe: Ill: The Free Press, 1953, p. 50.

David E. Apter, *Introduction to Political Anaiysis,* Prentice Hall of India Pvt. Ltd., New Delhi, 1981, pp. 456-57.

David Pitt, *The Social Dynamics* of *Development,* Pergmon Press, 1976.

David W. Brokensha, D.M. Warren and Oswald Werner, eds., *Indigenous Systems of Knowledge and Development,* Lanham MD: University Press of America, Inc., 1980.

de Coninck, John. "Evaluating the Impact of NGO's in Rural Poverty Alleviation: Uganda Country Study." ODI working Paper No. 51, February, 1992.

Dennis F. Thompson, *The Democratic Citizens, Social Service and Democratic Theory in the 20th Century,* Cambridge, 1990, Chap. III.

DeSouza, A. (1775): Day Care Under Privileged Children: A Study of Creches in Delhi, in a edited book entitled "Children in India by the same author, Mohan Publication, Delhi.

Deull, Charles B. and Laurel A. Dutcher. *Working Together: NGO Cooperation in Seven African Countries*. New York: Interaction 1987.

Dichter, Thomas W. "The Changing World of Northern NGOs: Problems, Paradoxes and Possibilities" in *Tansnational Associations* 2, 1991. pp. 66-70.

Dreze, Jean and Amartya Sen ,(1995). *India: Economic Development and Social Opportunity,* Delhi: Oxford University Press.

Edwards, Michael and David Hulme, *Making a difference: NGOs and Development in a Changing World.* London: Earthscan, 1992

Edwards, Michael. 1991. Strengthening Government Capacity for National Development and International Negotiation. London: Save the Children Fund.

Eldridge, Philip (1984/5). 'The political role of community action groups in India and Indonesia: In search of a general theory', *Alternatives* 10, pp. 401-34.

Elliott, Charles. 1987. "Some Aspects of Relations Between North and South in the NGO Sector." World Development 15(Supplement): 57-68.

Esman, Milton J. and Norman Uphoff. *Local Organizations: Intermediaries in Rural Development.* Ithaca: Cornell University Press, 1984.

Esquel Group Foundation. "Civil Society, State and Market: An Emerging Partnership for Equitable Development." Bethesda, January 1993.

Esquel Group Foundation. "Enabling Civil Society's Participation in Socio- economic Development in Latin America." Bethesda, 1993.

Fama, E. and M. Jensen (1994). 'Separation of ownership and control', *Journal of Law and Economics* 26, pp. 301-26.

Farrington, John and A. Bebbington. *Reluctant Partners? Nongovernmental Organizations, the State and Sustainable Agricultural Development.* London: Routledge, 1993.

Farrington, John et. al. (eds.). *Nongovernmental Organizations and the State in Asia.* London: Routledge, 1993.

Fernandes, Walter. *Voluntary Action and Government Control.* New Delhi: Indian Social Institute, 1986.

Fernandez, Aloysius. 1987. "NGOs in South Asia: People's Participation and Partnership." World Development 15(Supplement): 39-50.

First Five Year Plan — A Draft Outline, Government of India, New Delhi, 1951, p. 146, *Third Five Year Plan,* Government of India, New Delhi, 1961, pp. 292-93 and also the documents of following Five Year Plans.

Fowler, Alan, P. Campbell, P. and B. Pratt. *Institutional Development and NGOs in Africa: Policy Perspectives for European Development Agencies.* Oxford: INTRAC, 1992.

Fowler, Alan. 1992. "NGOs as Agents of Democratization: An African Perspective." Mimeo (draft). University of Sussex, Institute of Development Studies, May.

Fowler, Alan. *Non-governmental Organizations in Africa: Achieving Comparative Advantage in Relief and Microdevelopment*. IDS Discussion Paper No. 249. Brighton: Institute of Development Studies, 1988.

Fundacion Alternativa. "Las ONG's Ecuatorianas Frente al Fondo de Inversion Social del Ecuador." Quito, July 1992.

Garilao, Ernesto. 1987. "Indigenous NGOs as Strategic Institutions: Managing the Relationship with Government and Resource Agencies." World Development 15(Supplement): 113- 120.

Gezelius, Helena and David Millwood, "NGOs in Development and Participation in Practice" in *Tansnational Associations*, 5, 1991. pp. 278-291.

Global Environmental Facility. *Participation by Nongovernmental Organiza- tions in the Clobal Environment Facility*. Document GEF/PA/93/2. Washington: GEF, May 1993.

Gokhale, S.D. & Sohoni. N.K. (1979): Child in India, Child Welfare Research in India, Somaiya Pub. Pvt. Ltd. Mumbay, p. 24.

Gopal, Gita and Alexandre Marc. *Study of Procurement and Disbursement Issues in Projects with Community Participation.* Human Resources Division, Note No. 17. Washington: The World Bank, Africa Technical Department, 1994.

Gordon-Drabek, Anne. "Development Alternatives: The Challenge for NGOs — An Overview of the Issues" in *World Development*, Vol. 15, Supplement, 1987.

Haeuber, Richard. "The World Bank and Environmental Assessment: The Role of Nongovernmental Organizations" in *Environmental Impact Assessment Review*. Vol. 12, 1992, pp. 331-347.

Handy, Charles. *Understanding Voluntary Organizations.* London: Penguin Books, 1988.

Hanlon, Joseph. 1990. "New Missionaries in Mozambique." Mimeo. London.

Hans Daalder, "Parties, Elites, and Political Development in Western Europe,' in Giuseppe De Palma, ed., *Mass Politics in Industrial Societies,* Chicago, Markham Publishing Company, 1972, pp. 4-36.

Hansman, H. (1979/80). 'The role of non-profit enterprise', *Yale Law Journal* 89, pp. 835-901.

Hardgrave, Robert L., Jr and Stanley A. Kochanek (1986). *India: Government and Politics in a Developing Nation,* San Diego: Harcourt Brace.

Hari Mohan Mathur, *Administering Development in the Third World: Constraints and Choices,* New Delhi, Sage Publications, 1986, p. 19.

Heaver, Richard. *Reaching People at the Periphery: Can the Bank's Population, Health and nutrition Operations Do Better?* Washington: World Bank, April 1988.

Hentschel, Jesko. *Does Participation Cost the World Bank More? Emerging Evidence.* Paper presented at the World Bank Workshop on Participatory Development, May 1994.

Hill, Tony. *Northern NGOs and Africa's Development: Background, Issues and Challenges.* Paper prepared for the Workshop on Mobilizing the Informal Sector and NGOs for Recovery and Development. Abuja, 1990.

Hirono, Ryokichi. "How to Promote Trilateral Cooperation among Governments, NGOs and International Agencies", in *World NGO Symposium Nagoya Congress.* OISCA International Center, 1987.

Hirsch, P. 1994. "Where Are the Roots of Thai Environmentalism?" TEI Quarterly Environmental Journal, Vol. 2, No. 2, April-June, pp. 5-15. Thailand Environmental Institute, Bangkok.

Hirschman, Albert 0. *Getting Ahead Collectively: Grassroots Experiences in Latin America*. New York: Pergamon Press, 1984.

Holloway, Richard. "Doing Development — Government, NGOs and the Rural Poor in Asia." CUSO, 1987.

Hulme, David and Michael Edwards, eds. 1992. Making a Difference? NGOs and Development in a Changing World. London: Earthscan.

Hursh-Cesar, Gerald et. al. *Development Effectiveness of Private Voluntary Organizations.* Washington, 1986.

Indian Journal of Public Administration (1987). Special number on 'Voluntary organisations and development: Their role', July-September.

Jain, Devaki (1956).'Struggle against power: Notes on Indian political behavior', *World Politics 7,* pp. 393-96.

Jhunjhunwala, Bharat (1986). 'Voluntary work as countervailing power', *Economic and Political Weekly* 21.

Johnson, W. and V. Johnson. *West Africa Governments and Volunteer Development Organizations: Priorities for Partnership.* Lanham: University Press of America, 1990.

K.K. Mukherjee, *Emerging Social Changes and Voluntary Organisations: Challenges and Responses,* Gram Niyojan Kendra, Ghaziabad, 1994.

Karat, Prakash (1984). 'Action groups/voluntary organisations: A factor in imperialist strategy', *The Marxist,* April-June, pp. 19-54.

Kari Deutsch, *Social Mobilization and Political Development,* pp. 493-514.

Kearns, J and J. Edgerton, *Participatory Project Planning.* Paper prepared for the World Bank Workshop on Participatory Development, May 1994.

Kochanck, Stanley A. (1974). *Business and Politics in India.* Berkeley: University of California Press.

Korten, David C. (1986). 'Micro-policy reforms: The role of

private voluntary agencies', working paper no. 12, The National Association of Schools of Public Administration, Washington; D.C.

Korten, David, "Third Generation NGO Strategies: A Key to People-Centered Development". *World Development*, October 1987.

Korten, David. *Getting to the 21st Century: Voluntary Action and Global Agenda*. West Hartford: Kumarian Press, 1989.

Korten, David. *Micropolicy Reform: the Role of Private Voluntary Agencies*. Working Paper No. 12 of the National Association of Schools of Public Administration (NASPAA). Washington: NASPAA, 1986.

Kothari, Smitu (1993). 'Social movements and the redefinition of democracy' in Philip Oldenburg (ed.), *India Briefing*. Boulder, CO: Westview Press, p. 142.

Lalita, N.V. (1975): Voluntary Work in India: A study of Volunteers in Welfare Agencies, NIPCCD, New Delhi, p. 204

Lalitha, N.V. and Kohli. M. (1982): Status of voluntary Efforts in Social Welfare: NIPCDD New Delhi, p. 15.

Landim, Leilah. "NGOs in Latin America" in *World Development*, Vol. 15, 1987.

Lissner, Jorgen. *The Politics of Altruism: A Study of the Political Behaviour of Voluntary Development Agencies*. Geneva: Lutheran World Federation, 1977.

Lucian Pye, *Politics, Personality and National-builiding,* New Haven, Yale University Press, 1962,

Mare, Alexandre and Gita Gopal. "Procurement and Disbursement." Draft paper prepared for the World Bank Workshop on Participatory Development, May 1994.

Mare, Alexandre. 1992. "NGOs in Kyrghyzstan." Mimeo. World Bank.

Marx, Karl (1983). 'Theses on. Feuerbach' in Eugene Kamenka (ed.). *The Portable KartMarx.* New York: Viking;.

Milton Esman. 'Politics in Development Administration" in John D. Montgomery and William J. Siffin. eds., *Approaches to Development: Politics, Administration and Change,* New York, McGraw Hill Co., 1966, p. 63.

Mitra, Subrata Kumar (1991). 'Crisis and resilience in Indian democracy', *International Social Science Journal* 43, p. 565.

Muir, Ann "Evaluating The Impact of NGOs in Rural Poverty Alleviation: Zimbabwe Country Study." ODI Working Paper No. 52. February, 1992.

Mumtaz Soysal, *Public Relations in Administration:.* II. The Influence of the Public on the Operation of Public Administration on excluding Electoral Rights, Brussels, International Institute of Administrative Sciences, 1966, pp 25-80.

Nagle, William and Sanjoy Ghose. *Community Participation in World Bank — Supported Projects.* Strategic Planning and Review Discussion Paper No. 8. Washington: World Bank, June 1990.

NGLS. *NGOs and Structural Adjustment.* United Nations NGO Liaison Service NGLS Occasional Paper No. 3. Geneva, April 1987.

Noorjahan Bava, *People's Participation in Development Administration in India,* New Delhi, Uppal Publishing House, 1984, p. 3.

Noorjahan Bava, *People's Participation, op. cit.,* p. 22.

Norton, Andrew and Thomas Stephens. *Participation in Poverty Assessments.* Draft paper prepared for the World Bank Workshop on Participatory Development, May 1994.

NOVIB. Banking on the Environment: *Vision of NGOs on Social and Environmental Aspects of Projects and Programmes of the World Bank.* The Hague, August 1990.

OEF International, "Women, Water and Development in Mexico: A Case Study of NGO Collaboration in a World Bank Project." Mimeo. Washington: OEF International, 1990.

Organization for Economic Cooperation and Development (OECD). 1988. Voluntary Aid for Development: The Role of NGOs. OECD: Paris.

Organization for Economic Cooperation and Development. *Voluntary Aid for Development — The Role of NGOs.* Paris: OECD, 1988.

P.D. Kulkarni, *Voluntary Action — The Myth and Reality,* NIPCCD, New Delhi, 1984, p. 4.

PACT. "The Negotiation of the Guatemalan Social Fund: An NGO Perspective." Mimeo, 1990.

Pandey, Shashi Ranjan (1991). *Community Action for Social Justice: Grassroots Organization in India.* New Delhi: Sage Publications.

Patel, Rohini (1995). 'The pressure group role of voluntary associations: A case study of the Ahmedabad's Women's Action Group and the Self-Employed

Women's Association,' unpublished Ph.D. dissertation, Pennsylvania State University.

Paul, Samuel R Arturo Israel (eds). *Nongovernmental Organizations and the World Bank: Cooperation for Development. World Bank Regional and Sectoral Studies.* Washington: The World Bank, 1991.

Paul, Samuel. *Community Participation in Development Projects: The World Bank Experience.* World Bank Discussion Paper No. 6. Washington: World Bank, 1987.

Paul, Samuel. *Govoernments and Grassroots Organizations: From Coexistence to Collaboration.* Washington: The World Bank, March 1988.

Pfirrmann, C. and Kron, D. 1992. Environment and NGOs in Thailand. Thai NGO Support Project and Friedrich-Naumann-Stiftung Foundation, Bangkok.

Poona Wignaraja, 'Towards a Theory and Practice of Rural Development', *Development and Change,* 1984, 2-3-11, p. 7.

Qureshi, Moeen. 1990. "The World Bank and NGOs: New Approaches." Speech to the Washington Chapter of the Society for International Development. April 22, 1990. World Bank, Washington, D.C.

R.L. Peabody, "Public Bureaucracies", in J.C. March, ed., *Handbook of Organization,* Chicago, and McNally College Publishing, 1965.

Rajashekar, D, M.K. Bhat and Neil Webster, *People Centered Rural Development: NGDOs and decentralized Government.* Bangalore: ISEC, CDS, BCO and NOVIB, 1995.

Ramachandran, Vimala (1996). 'NGOs in the time of globalisation', *Seminar,* November.

Ridell, Roger. "Judging Success: Evaluating NGO Approaches to Alleviating Poverty in Developing Countries." ODI Working Paper No. 37, May, 1990.

Ruland, J. and Ladavalya, B. 1991. "Voluntary Associations and Municipal Government in Thailand." Report submitted to the Foundation Volkswagenwerk, Hannover, the Federal Republic of Germany.

Saint, Kishore (1974). 'The role of the catalyst institution' in John Sommer, Pratima Kale and Ranjit Gupta (eds), *Rural Development at the Grassroots: The Catalyst Role.* New Delhi: Ford Foundation.

Salamon, Lester and Helmut Anheier. *In Search of the Nonprofit Sector II: The Problem of Classification.* Working Paper of the Johns Hopkins Comparative Nonprofit Sector Project, 1992.

Salisburg, Robert (1969). 'An exchange theory of interest groups', *Midwest Journal of Political Science* 13, no. I, pp. 1-32.

Salmen, Lawrence and Paige Eaves. *World Bank Work with Nongovernmental Organizations.* Country Economics Department Working Paper No. 305. Washington: World Bank, December 1989.

Samuel P. Huntington and Joan M. Nelson, *No Easy Choice: Political Participation in Developing Countries,* Cambridge, Mass: Harvard University Press, 1976, p. 1.

Samuel Paul, *Strategic Management of Development Programmes,* Geneva, ILO, 1983, p. 95.

Sen, K.M. (1961). *Hinduism.* Baltimore: Penguin Books.

Sethi, Harsh (1985). 'Whither voluntary action?', *Seminar,* May, pp. 18-23.

Seymour Martin Lipset, *Politics and The Social Sciences,* New Delhi, Anand R. Kundaji for Wiley Eastern Pvt. Ltd., 1972, p. xiii.

Shah, Dinesh (1985). 'Voluntary agencies in the seventh plan', *Voluntary Action* 27, nos 9-10, p. 259.

Shah, Ghanshyam and H.R. Chaturvedi (1983). *Gandhian Approach to Rural Development: The Valod Experiment.* New Delhi: Ajanta.

Sharma, S.L. (1992). 'Social action groups as harbingers of silent revolution', *Economic and Political Weekly* 27, pp. 2557-61.

Sheth, D.L. (1983/4). "Grass-roots stirring and the future of polities', *Alternatives* 9, pp. 1-24.

Sheth, D.L. and Harsh Sethi (1991). 'The NGO sector in India: Historical context and current discourse', Voluntas 2, p. 51.

Sidel, M. 1994. "The Emergence of a Non-profit Sector and Philanthropy in the Socialist Republic of Vietnam." Prepared for the Survey on Non- governmental Underpinnings of the Emerging Asia-Pacific Regional Community

Sills, D.L. (Ed.), *International Encyclopedia of Social Sciences,* Vol. 15, New York, The Macmillan and The Free Press, 1972, pp. 362-63.

Smillie, Ian and Henry Helmich, *Non-Governmental Organizations and Governments: Stakeholders for development*. Development Centre. Paris: OECD, 1993.

Smillie, Ian. *A Time to Build Up: New Forms of Cooperation Between NGOs and CIDA.* Ottawa: Canadian Council for International Cooperation, December 1991.

Smith, Derek. *Study of the Role of United Kingdom NGOs in Providing Development Aid.* Washington: The World Bank, July 1987.

Sollis, Peter. "Multilateral Agencies and NGOs in the Context of Policy Reform." Unpublished paper presented to the Conference on Changing U.S. and Multilat- eral Policy toward Central America organized by the Washington Office on Latin America (WOLA), Washington, June 10 to June 12, 1991.

Stearns, Katherine and Marie Otero. *The Critical Connection: Governments, Private Institutions, and the Informal Sector in Latin America.* ACCION International Monograph Series No. 5. Washington: ACCION, August 1990.

Steckhan, Rainer. 1990. Memo to Alexander Shakow re: Response to Brown Paper "Policy Impacts on the NGO Sector." April 10. World Bank, Washington, D.C.

Stevulak, Catharine and Anne Thompson. "Approaches to Bank/NGO Collaboration." Mimeo. Washington, 1993.

Tandon, Rajesh. *The Relationship between NGOs and Government.* Mimeo paper presented to the Conference on the Promotion of Autonomous Development. New Delhi: PRIA, 1987.

Tandon, Yash. "Foreign NGOs, Uses an Abuses: An African Perspective", in *IFDA Dossier* 81, April/June 1991.

Tendler, Judith. *Turning Private Voluntary Organizations into Development Agencies: Questions for Evaluation,* AID Program Evaluation Discussion Paper No. 12. Washington: USAID, 1982.

There is a great variety of NGOs. For typology of these see N.R. Inamdar, "Role of Voluntarism in Development" and V.G. Nandekar, "Voluntary Association — A Strategy in Development", *The Indian Journal of Public Administration,* Special Number on Voluntary Functions, July-Sept. 1987, Vol. XXXIII. No. 3.

Thomson, Ann. "Working with the World Bank." Mimeo. Ottawa: CARE- Canada, 1993.

UN, *Decentralization far National and Local Development,* New York, Division of Public Administration. Department of Economic and Social Affairs, Sales No. UN Publications, 62 HH 2, p. 32.

United Nations, *Popular Participation in Decision-making for Development,* New York, UN Department of Economic and Social Affairs, 1975. Also See Lothar A. Kotzch, "People's Participation as a Task of Planning" (Nepal) *Development and Cooperation,* No. 3, May-June 1984, pp. 24-25.

Uphoff, Norman. 1987. "Relations between Government and NGOs and the Promotion of Autonomous Development." Paper presented to the Conference on the Promotion of Autonomous Development. Cornell University, Ithaca, N.Y.

V.A. Thompson, "Bureaucracy in a Democratic Society", in Roscoe Martin, ed., *Public Administration and Democracy,* Syracuse, 1965.

VanDomelen, Julie. "Working with Nongovernmental Organizations," in S. Jorgensen et. al. (eds), *Bolivia's Answer to Poverty, Economic Crisis, and Adjustment: The Emergency Social Fund.* World Bank Regional and Sectoral Studies. Washington: World Bank, 1992.

Viswanath, Vanita (1991). *Nongovemmtntal Organizations and Women's Development in South Asia: A Comparative Analysis.* Boulder, Co: Westview Press.

Viswanath, Vanita and Michael Bamberger. *Issues and Opportunities for Expanded NGO Participation in National Development Policies and Programs.* Paper prepared for the BRAC/EDI Workshop on Livestock. Washington: World Bank, Economic Development Institute.

Voorhies, Samuel J. *Working with Government using World Bank Funds: Learnings from the Uganda Orphans and Health Rehabilitation Program.* World Vision Staff Working Paper No. 16. Monrovia: World Vision, 1993.

Webster, Neil, "The Role of NGDOs in Indian Rural Development: Some Lessons from West Bengal and Karnataka". Copenhagen: Centre for Development Research, 1993.

Wellard, Kate and J. Copestake (eds.). *Nongovernmental Organizations and the State in Africa.* London: Routledge, 1993.

Williams, Aubrey. "A Growing Role for NGOs in Development" in *Finance and Development*, December 1990.

World Bank. "Encouraging Private Contributions to African Development." Paper presented at the Enabling Environment Conference. Nairobi, October 1986.

World Bank. *50th Anniversary: Working with NGOs.* Insert in World Bank 50th Anniversary Information Packet, 1994.

World Bank. *Cooperation Between the World Bank and NGOs, Annual Progress Report*. Washington: World

Bank, Operations Policy Group, NGO Unit, 1990 to present.

World Bank. *Environment Assessment Sourcebook: Vol. I, II, III.* Washington: World Bank, 1991.

World Bank. *How the World Bank Works with Nongovernmental Organizations.* Washington: World Bank, 1990.

World Bank. *Poverty Reduction Handbook*, Washington: World Bank, 1992.

World Bank. *Republic of Uganda: The Role of Nongovernmental Organizations and Country Based Groups in Poverty Alleviation*, Report No. 12262-VG. Washington: World Bank: Eastern Africa Department, Population and Human Resources Division, September, 1993.

World Bank. *Socioeconomic Development Funds: A Guideline for Design and Implementation.* Washington: World Bank, Africa Region, Social Dimensions of Adjustment and Development Unit February 1991.

World Bank. *Strengthening the Role of Nongovernmental Organizations in the Health and Family Welfare Program in India.* Washington: World Bank, Asia Country Department, Population and Human Resources, June 18, 1990.

World Bank. *Sustainability of projects First Review of Experience*. Washington: World Bank, Operations Evaluation Department, June 14, 1985.

World Bank. *The World Bank and Participation.* Washington: The World Bank, Operations Policy Department, September, 1994.

World Bank, *Zambia — Lusaka Squatter Upgrading Site and Services Project*, Project Completion Report, June 30, 1993.

Wriner, Myron (1991). 'The Indian paradox: Violent social conflict and democratic polities' in S.N. Eisenstadt *(ed.), Democracy and Modernity.* Leiden: E. J. Brill, pp. 69-85.

Index

J

K

L

M

N

O

P